THE TREE ARMY

A PICTORIAL HISTORY OF THE

CIVILIAN CONSERVATION CORPS

1933 - 1942

UNITED STATES · CIVILIAN CONSERVATION CORPS

CCC

THE TREE ARMY

A PICTORIAL HISTORY OF THE
CIVILIAN CONSERVATION CORPS, 1933-1942.

By STAN COHEN

Camp Harry Hopkins, Beverly Hills, California. Hopkins was President Roosevelt's chief advisor during the Depression years.

Pictorial Histories Publishing Company
Missoula, Montana

LIBRARY OF CONGRESS
CATALOG CARD NO. 80-81071

ISBN 0-933126-11-5

First Printing: June 1980
Fourth Printing: April 1991

REVISED EDITION
First Printing: April 1993
Second Printing: January 1996
Third Printing: March 1998
Fourth Printing: March 1999
Fifth Printing: March 2001
Sixth Printing: March 2003
Seventh Printing: May 2004
Eighth Printing: March 2005
Ninth Printing: March 2006
Tenth Printing: January 2007
Eleventh Printing: January 2008

COVER ART Monte Dolack, Missoula, Montana
PRINTED BY Jostens, Visalia, California

COVER PHOTOGRAPH
Since the first printing of this book in 1980 the name of the
CCC "boy" on the cover was unknown. In May 2007 his identity
was discovered—William J. Rankinen.

PICTORIAL HISTORIES PUBLISHING CO., INC.
713 South Third Street West, Missoula, MT 59801
PHONE (406) 549-8488, FAX (406) 728-9280
EMAIL phpc@montana.com
WEBSITE pictorialhistoriespublishing.com

⏫ PREFACE ⏫

*T*he decade 1933-1943 was a critical period in American history. The Civilian Conservation Corps (CCC) played a big part in bringing our country and its people back to normal during those difficult times.

The billions of trees planted, the millions of acres of land reclaimed; the parks, bridges, dams and fire trails built; plus all the other projects are still much in evidence today.

Equally important, the CCC took millions of unemployed young men off the streets, gave them hope, helped them to be self-supporting and build self-respect and taught them how to be men. Many learned to read and write, obtained diplomas, or learned a trade. A large percentage served their country honorably and with distinction in World War II. Most went on to be outstanding citizens and a credit to their country and communities. The CCC will always be close to the hearts of those helped by it.

The experience gained and the benefits derived during the nine years of the CCC should be studied carefully. This unique program coped successfully with a grave national problem which, some 60 years later, is once again a source of great national concern.

About four million Americans—mostly male—were associated with the CCC. Today, about two million are still with us and the majority are part of the growing Senior Citizen population. They are increasingly concerned about the mounting problems facing both young and Senior Americans. They are still concerned about the depletion and abuse of our country's natural resources.

This is why, six decades later, those associated with the CCC are building the National Association of CCC Alumni. These gray heads, through organized effort, intend to revive, and preserve the comradeship, nostalgia, history and accomplishments of the CCC while at the same time, doing something tangible to solve today's problems.

ROBERT L. GRIFFITHS
co-founder National Association of
Civilian Conservation Corps Alumni

OATH OF ENROLLMENT

(Upon entering the CCC, each enrollee subscribed to the following oath. It is a contract between the enrollee and the U. S. Government, and should be lived up to in each respect.)

I, —————————, do solemnly swear that the information given above as to my status is correct. I agree to remain in the Civilian Conservation Corps for the period terminating at the discretion of the United States between ——————— unless sooner released by proper authority, and that I will obey those in authority and observe all the rules and regulations thereof to the best of my ability and will accept such allowances as may be provided pursuant to law and regulations promulgated pursuant thereto. I understand and agree that any injury received or disease contracted by me while a member of the Civilian Conservation Corps cannot be made the basis of any claim against the government, except such as I may be entitled to under the act of September 7, 1916, and that I shall not be entitled to any allowances upon release from camp, except transportation in kind to the place at which I was accepted for enrollment. I understand further that any articles issued to me by the United States Government for use while a member of the Civilian Conservation Corps are, and remain, property of the United States Government and that willful destruction, loss, sale or disposal of such property renders me financially responsible for the cost thereof and liable to trial in the civil courts. I understand further that any infraction of the rules or regulations of the Civilian Conservation Corps renders me liable to expulsion therefrom. So help me God.

⇑ INTRODUCTION ⇑

When I began my research for this book, I did not understand the complexities of the Civilian Conservation Corps, or realize the magnitude of the effect it had on American life in its nine-year history. I was vaguely familiar with the organization, I knew it had helped build the park system in my native state of West Virginia, and had contributed to parks elsewhere in the country.

But I did not know that more than three million men had been involved, or that more than 4,000 camps had been established—not only in every one of the then 48 states, but also in Alaska, Hawaii, Puerto Rico, and the Virgin Islands. The CCC was truly national in character. In the opinion of many people, it was the best and most productive of the New Deal agencies. Some even say that the CCC won World War II. That may be an exaggeration, but it is true that in the dark days of 1941 and 1942 the CCC provided a vast pool of trained officers for the Army, plus more than three million men who had experienced military-style living and job training.

Good books have been written on the history of the Corps, and the experiences of men who served in it.

I have not tried to duplicate these efforts. Instead, I have tried through pictures to show how the enrollees lived and worked. From thousands of photographs, I have chosen those that I believe best represent the concept and spirit of the Corps.

After spending nearly a year on this project and talking to many men who were involved with the CCC, I am firmly convinced that it was a noble idea that came along at just the right time in the history of our country, and that its legacy is still with us today. Times have changed in 60 years. Maybe, though, the concept of the Civilian Conservation Corps, updated, could be of service to America again.

To you men who served in the Tree Army, I hope this book brings back memories. You of newer generations, I hope this book contributes to appreciation of the times your parents and grandparents lived through in the 1930s. To all you who read this, I hope this book tells something of the magnificent work the Corps did in the building, protection, and development of our natural resources.

STAN COHEN
Missoula, Montana

♠ ACKNOWLEDGMENTS ♠

Many people throughout the United States helped with this project, during the initial writing in 1981 and with this revised edition in 1993. Without them this book could not have been completed.

I am deeply indebted to the personnel of the National Association of Civilian Conservation Corps Alumni (NACCCA), especially its co-founder Robert Griffiths and its present president, Lloyd Mielke. Through the association and its newsletter, I received information, photographs and artifacts from CCC alumni throughout the country. This organization has kept the spirit of the CCC alive.

Jud Moore of the U.S. Forest Service regional office in Missoula, Montana, helped obtain the numerous Forest Service photographs used in this book. Officials of other Forest Service regional and local offices were cooperative, as were employees of the National Park Service offices.

Individuals who provided help include: Martin Cole of Whittier, California, who sent his photo collection and several stories used; Bill Sharp of Missoula, Montana, who has compiled the entire history of the CCC in the state; Ken Steeber of Shenandoah National Park Archives, who opened the extensive photo files of the park to me; Charles "Moon" Mullens of Edinburg, Virginia, a key player in the Camp Roosevelt story; Larry Sypolt of Morgantown, West Virginia, an avid collector of CCC memorabilia; and Don Hobart of Sacramento, California, Roy Marker of Marienville, Pennsylvania, Edward Rosen of St. Petersburg, Florida, Bill McNeel of Marlinton, West Virginia, Susanne Levitsky, California Conservation Corps, Rudy Polise, Pensacola, Florida, and personnel of the Chippewa National Forest, Ninemile Ranger Station, Lolo National Forest, Petrified Forest National Park and La Purisima Mission State Park.

My thanks to Bob McGiffert of Missoula for editing my manuscript, Nancy Ferko, who typed the manuscript and Joan Fox for proofreading it. And a final thanks to all the people who put up with my ramblings about the CCC and about a period of American history most were not familiar with.

The photographs and artifacts were gathered from various sources throughout the United States. Sources are as follows:

USFS — United States Forest Service
NA — National Archives
LC — Library of Congress
UPI — United Press International
NACCCA — National Association of CCC Alumni
Other sources are acknowledged individually.
Photos not credited are from the author's collection.

⇑ TABLE OF CONTENTS ⇑

President Franklin Delano Roosevelt, father of the CCC.

SOCIETY DOYERS ST.

GOSPEL

Scenes like this were characteristic of the early years of the

When Franklin D. Roosevelt accepted the Democratic presidential nomination in 1932, he made this statement—one which was to change forever the politics of the United States: "I pledge you, I pledge myself, to a new deal for the American people."

The great depression, begun with the stock market crash of October 1929, had by 1932 shattered the prosperity most Americans enjoyed during the 1920s. Millions were jobless and business was at a standstill. An estimated 12 million to 15 million people—one worker out of every four—were out of work. Many had lost homes and farms because they could not meet mortgage payments.

Herbert Hoover was renominated by the Republican Party in 1932 but economic conditions left him with little chance to keep his job as president. Roosevelt won 472 electoral votes to Hoover's 59, and when the new president took office on March 4, 1933, he had a mandate to revitalize the economy and end the depression.

By then, the depression had hit bottom. There were bread lines in the cities. Banks had failed. Houses and farms had been abandoned. Men who formerly had supported families were going door to door, begging for food, for shoes, for dimes. To add to the misery, natural disasters were creating great dust bowls in the Midwest. Because there was no conservation policy the country was being drained of its abundant natural resources.

Roosevelt's first act upon becoming president was to declare a bank holiday on March 6, 1933. He closed all banks in the country until Treasury Department officials could check the stability of them. Banks found to be in good financial condition were supplied with money and allowed to reopen. Others simply closed for good. This action stopped bank "runs" by panicky depositors who had rushed to withdraw their money and gold.

Congress was called into special session on March 5 to work on emergency bills. Thus began the "Hundred Days" that were to produce much legislation still in force today, and many agencies and programs made famous by initials: NRA, FDIC, AAA, PWA, HOLC, TVA, FCA, CCC and many more.

The NRA was the National Recovery Administration, established to enforce codes of fair practice for business and industry. It proved to be too radical for the people, and the act creating it was declared unconstitutional in 1935 by the Supreme Court. The FDIC, the Federal Deposit Insurance Corporation, initially insured bank deposits up to $2,500. The AAA, the Agricultural Adjustment Administration, regulated farm production. The PWA, the Public Works Administration, provided jobs and purchasing power through construction projects. The HOLC, the Home Owners Loan Corporation, granted long-term mortgage loans at low interest. The TVA, the Tennessee Valley Authority, helped develop the resources of the Tennessee Valley by building dams for flood protection and electrical power. The FCA, the Farm Credit Administration, provided long-term and short-term credit to farmers. The CCC, the Civilian Conservation Corps, put unemployed youths to work revitalizing natural resources.

These agencies and others vastly increased the influence of the government on the everyday life of Americans. The FCC, the Federal Communications Commission (1934), regulated the radio and telegraph industry; the FHA, the Federal Housing Administration (1934), insured home loans to private lending agencies; the FSA, the Farm Security Administration (1937), helped farmers buy equipment; the NLRB, the National Labor Relations Board (1935), administered the National Labor Relations Act; the NYA, the National Youth Administration (1935), provided jobs training for unemployed youths; the REA, the Rural Electrification Administration (1935), brought power to farms; the SEC, the Securities and Exchange Commission (1934), regulated stock market practices; the SSB, the Social Security Board (1935), set up the present Social Security System; the WPA, the Works Progress Administration (1935), provided projects for needy people.

The New Deal affected every man, woman, and child in the United States. It showed the world that a democracy could rescue itself from a terrible financial disaster without resorting to the authoritarian politics of dictatorship. Even so, it took a war to restore full employment and financial stability.

Headlines in newspapers around the country heralded a new era in American politics and economics in March 1933.

The Depression affected literally every family in the United States. The Civilian Conservation Corps was just one of the governmental programs attempting to alleviate the suffering.

Enrollees arriving at the
Jefferson Barracks,
Missouri, conditioning
camp in April 1933. NA

INITIAL
ORGANIZATION

The Civilian Conservation Corps was not an idea that occurred to the Democratic presidential candidate, Franklin Delano Roosevelt, in 1932. He had been a conservationist for many years and as governor of New York, had put some of the later CCC concepts into practice. It was clear to Roosevelt that something drastic had to be done about unemployment of youth and the waste of natural resources.

By 1932 more than 5 million young men were unemployed, and World War I veterans in huge numbers were also without jobs. These men roamed the country looking for work, went on the welfare rolls, or turned to crime.

Millions of acres of farm land were being eroded. Millions more were being threatened by fire or by indiscriminate timber harvesting. Recreational opportunities were being lost because of budget and personnel problems.

Two days after Roosevelt's inauguration on March 4, 1933, the new president called a meeting of high government officials to create a Civilian Conservation Corps. Attending were the secretaries of War, Agriculture, and Interior, the director of the Bureau of the Budget, the Judge Advocate General of the Army, and the solicitor of the Department of the Interior.

Roosevelt's plan was to put up to 500,000 unemployed youths to work in forests, parks, and range lands.

The Army would run the camps. The agriculture and interior departments would be responsible for work projects and provide the personnel to manage them. The budget director would provide the financial assistance and the solicitor and judge advocate would offer legal advice. The Department of Labor would coordinate the selection of enrollees. Roosevelt stressed the importance of speed. The government officials said they could do the job.

On March 21, the President sent a message to the 73rd Congress on the establishment of the organization:

> I propose to create a Civilian Conservation Corps to be used in simple work, not interfering with normal employment, and confining itself to forestry, the prevention of soil erosion, flood control, and similar projects.
>
> More important, however, than the material gains, will be the moral and spiritual value of such work. The overwhelming majority of unemployed Americans, who are now walking the streets and receiving private or public relief would infinitely prefer to work. We can take a vast army of these unemployed out into healthful surroundings. We can eliminate to some extent at least the threat that enforced idleness brings to spiritual and moral stability. It is not a panacea for all the unemployment, but it is an essential step in this emergency . . .

Robert Fechner, director of the CCC from 1933 to 1939.
NACCCA

> I estimate that 250,000 men can be given temporary employment by early summer if you will give me the authority to proceed within the next two weeks.

Roosevelt got the go-ahead from Congress on March 31. He had full authority to proceed at his discretion to establish the CCC.

Rather than establish a new federal bureaucracy, the President used the existing War, Agriculture, Interior and Labor departments. The organization was first called Emergency Conservation Work, but the name used by Roosevelt in his congressional speech, Civilian Conservation Corps, was the popular one. Not until 1937, however, was the name made official by Congress.

Roosevelt's friend, Robert Fechner, a Boston labor leader, was tapped to head the new organization. He had a long career in the American labor movement and was to prove a capable director. (His assistant, James J. McEntee, a labor leader from New Jersey, assumed the directorship upon Fechner's death in 1940.)

A CCC Advisory Council was established, composed of representatives of the War, Agriculture, Interior, and Labor departments.

Thirty-seven days elapsed between Roosevelt's inauguration and the signing of the first enrollee on April 7, 1933. Henry Rich of Alexandria, Virginia, was sent to Camp Roosevelt near Luray, Virginia. A miracle of cooperation among government agencies had occurred. Even mobilization during World War I did not match the CCC effort.

The initial call was for 250,000 "boys" to be enrolled by July 1, 1933. They were to be unemployed, between 18 and 25 years old and unmarried. They were to come from families on relief. Men from every part of the country, from cities and farms, signed up and they were sent

This is to notify you that your son (~~brother~~) (~~ward~~) has been accepted for enrollment in the Civilian Conservation Corps and has been sent to Company No. _____
at _____ _____, Minn.

Should you change your address, notification of such change should be sent to:

Commanding Officer,

Company _____ , CCC,

_____ , Minn.

Allotment check will be mailed so as to reach you on or about the 10th of each month. Do not telephone or write in regard to check until after that date.

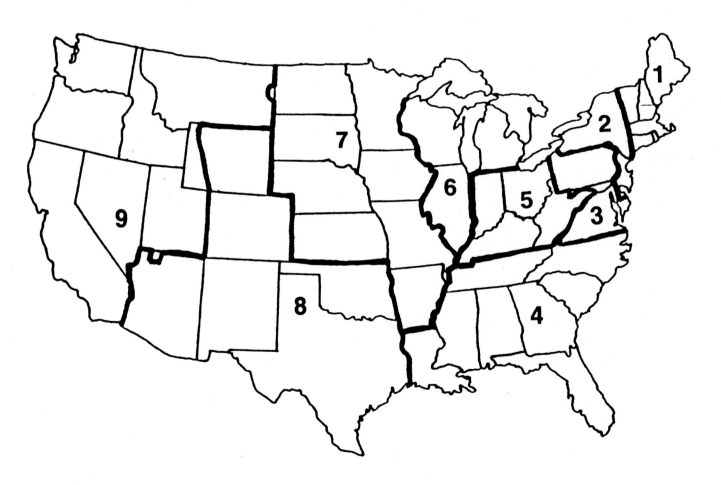

Nine Army Corps Areas directing the Civilian Conservation Corps.

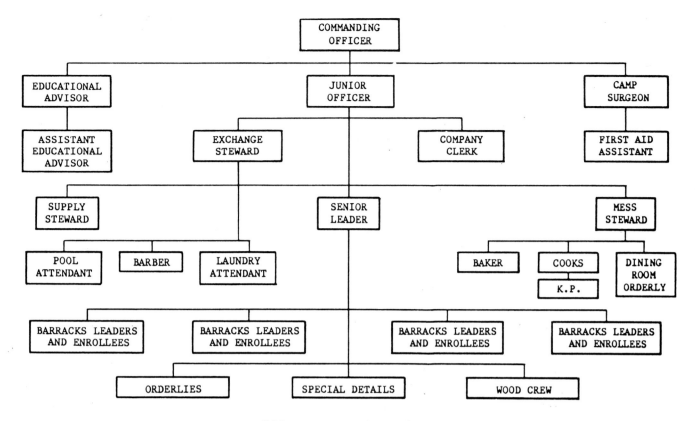

CCC company organization chart.

to every part of the country. On April 14, enrollment of 14,000 Indians was authorized because of chronic unemployment and soil erosion on the reservations. These men stayed on their reservations and lived at home under the jurisdiction of the Office of Indian Affairs. On April 22, enrollment of 24,000 "Local Experienced Men," or "L.E.M." was authorized. These usually were older men who had experience in woodcraft and were hired to supervise the work crews. The Forest Service, which was responsible for most of the camp projects, did not have the manpower to manage the thousands of youths enrolling. On May 11, 24,000 veterans of World War I, men in their 30's and 40's, were authorized for enrollment. Due to severe unrest and unemployment among the veterans, especially during the Bonus Army trouble of 1932, a partial solution to the problems was the enrollment of veterans in their own conservation camps.

The enlistment period was six months with the option of re-enlistment for another six months up to a maximum of two years. The enrollee was paid $30 a month, of which $25 was sent to his family. The remaining $5 could be used by the enrollee at the camp canteen or for personal expenses of his choice. Room, board, clothing and tools were provided by the government. The enrollee was expected to work a 40-hour week and adhere to camp rules.

The pay of $30 a month, or $1 a day, was opposed by labor organizations as too low. But the wage was mainly an instrument to get the thousands of unemployed off the streets and into productive work.

By May, it was obvious that the President's call for 250,000 enrollees by July 1 would not be met, and on May 12 an executive order was issued in a bid to clear up some of the misunderstandings that had developed among the cooperating agencies. It had the desired effect. By July 4, approximately 275,000 youths, L.E.M., Indians and veterans were enrolled in the CCC.

Initially the enrollees were sent to conditioning camps at existing army bases. Here the enrollees went through days of exercise before being sent to their assigned camps. The War Department ran the camps and by July 1, the Army had 3,000 regular Army officers, 1,890 reserve officers, 556 Navy and Marine officers, and 300 contract surgeons on active duty, supervising CCC operations.

Except for a few installations in Northern states, camps were racially segregated: white, Negro and Indian. An effort was made to integrate the camps for war veterans, but it did not work out.

Nearly 200,000 blacks were enrolled during the life of the CCC. Several camps for women were reported to have been established in New Hampshire and New York, but the CCC was mainly a man's organization.

The first camp was established in the George Washington National Forest near Luray, Virginia, and was

officially occupied on April 17, 1933. It was designated successively as Camp GWNF-1, NF-1, F-1 and Camp Roosevelt. It was recognized as a historic site by the U.S. Forest Service in 1966.

Thus the CCC was well-established in 1933: 275,000 men encamped across the United States and in Alaska, Hawaii, Puerto Rico, and the Virgin Islands.

On July 17, 1933, President Roosevelt made a radio address to the CCC that typified his thoughts about the organization he had created. He said:

Men of the Civilian Conservation Corps, I think of you as a visible token of encouragement to the whole country. You—nearly 300,000 strong—are evidence that the nation is still strong enough and broad enough to look after its citizens.

You are evidence that we are seeking to get away as fast as we possibly can from soup kitchens and free rations, because the government is paying you wages and maintaining you for actual work—work which is needed now and for the future and will bring a definite financial return to the people of the nation.

Through you the nation will graduate a fine group of strong young men, clean-living, trained to self-discipline and, above all, willing and proud to work for the joy of working.

Too much in recent years large numbers of our population have sought out success as an opportunity to gain money with the least possible work.

It is time for each and every one of us to cast away self-destroying nation-destroying efforts to get something for nothing, and to appreciate that satisfying reward and safe reward come only through honest work.

That must be the new spirit of the American future.

You are the vanguard of that new spirit.

Setting up exercises at Camp Bullis, Texas, near San Antonio, 1933. NA

Recruits in their new blue denims stand inspection at the Ft. Sheridan, Illinois, conditioning center, 1933. NA

Mailing letters home from the Ft. Slocum, New York, conditioning camp, 1933. UPI

Conditioning exercises at Jefferson Barracks, Missouri,
1933. NA

THE FIRST CCC CAMP

The first CCC camp in the country was designated successively as Camp GWNF-1, F-1 and Camp Roosevelt. The 13-acre camp was located in the George Washington National Forest, Virginia, on Mt. Kennedy, nine miles southeast of Edinburg. It was in operation from April 17, 1933 to May 25, 1942, the entire period of CCC activity. The camp averaged 200 enrollees, drawn primarily from Virginia and the Washington D.C. area. Work projects included a variety of achievements: road building and maintenance, fish and wildlife management, forest culture and improvements, fire hazard reduction and recreational improvements. The camp site was recognized as a historic site by the U.S. Forest Service in 1966 and now serves as a Forest Service picnic area.

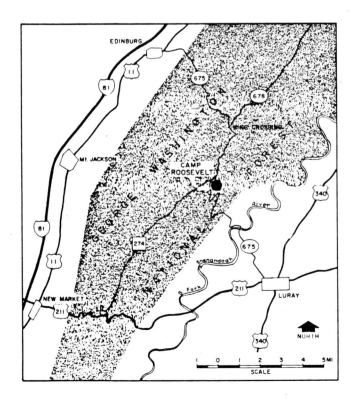

The first recruits of the CCC march through the woods to their camp at the first CCC camp near Edinburg, Virginia, in April 1933. UPI

Men arriving at Camp Roosevelt near Edinburg, Virginia, in April 1933. USFS

The first day at the first camp: April 18, 1933, Camp Roosevelt near Edinburg, Virginia, in the George Washington National Forest. USFS

An army bell or pyramid tent at Camp Roosevelt, George Washington National Forest, Virginia, 1933. Tents were used at new camps until barracks could be built. USFS

Entering the mess hall at Camp Roosevelt after evening retreat, 1940. NA

Education building at Camp Roosevelt, 1940. NA

Chow gang at Camp Roosevelt, 1940. NA

Building foundation remains at the former site of Camp Roosevelt.

Picnic shelter built by former CCC members from the surrounding area.

CHARLES MULLEN'S RECOLLECTIONS OF CAMP ROOSEVELT

Charles Mullens was living in Alberene, Va., when he joined the CCC in 1934. He was signed up at the welfare office in Charlottesville and from there went to Fort Monroe for shots and other camp preparations. From Fort Monroe he was sent to Camp Roosevelt by train to Edinburg and on by army truck to the camp. He recalled:

> You felt lonesome when you got over there in the mountains, but it so happened I knew three boys there who were from my home community. It took awhile to get accustomed and used to it, but the longer you stayed the better you liked it.

Mullens stayed for six years, first as an enrollee and later as an L.E.M.

When Mullens reached Camp Roosevelt, the five barracks were already built. The camp could hold 250 men at full capacity, but the number fluctuated as the men came and went. A typical day started with breakfast around 6:00 or 6:30. Barracks leaders would get their men ready and march them to mess halls. The men carried their mess kits with them and were served on a first-come, first-served basis. After breakfast they washed their kits in a tank of hot water and went back to their barracks to straighten things up and prepare for work. During the day, Mullens was a truck foreman. He recalled:

> They would send you across the road to the Forest Service and they would issue the tools for you to take, and tell you what truck to get on. . . . There'd be a telephone crew, road crew that you'd slope the banks. . . . On road crew you had a mound of shale [you'd] beat up to make the roads . . . go to the quarries, get the shale out, and some of the men would have to . . . blast the rock . . . and you shovel it on a truck, and they'd take you to spray it on the road.

Hot meals were trucked to enrollees working outside the camp. Meals were all prepared by enrollee cooks. At the end of the workday, the men would march to supper, stopping on the way for flag salute and mail call. After dinner there was a choice of recreational and educational activities. Two or three nights a week trucks would take enrollees to town.

Mullens remembers that work projects undertaken by Camp Roosevelt included firefighting, recreation area development, and construction of the Woodstock Tower. Mullens recalls the camp's participation in bringing deer back into the Shenandoah Valley. Deer were hauled in trucks from Pennsylvania and let loose in the Virginia mountains.

Mullens felt the communities nearby were glad to have the camp there, mostly because of the economic benefits it brought. Community relations were improved further through competitive athletics between the towns and Camp Roosevelt. Many enrollees also participated in local church activities. It was through the Edinburg church that Mullens met his future wife. Most of the camp's supplies were obtained locally, and local labor brought in to do any major building work.

Mullens feels that being a CCC taught him discipline, a quality he needed later in the army. It also taught him skills, such as using a saw and cutting wood, and how to get along with different kinds of people. Some time after Camp Roosevelt closed, the buildings were torn down and sold publicly. The water tanks and pump were cleaned up and used when the new recreation area was built over the old camp site.

Mullens married and settled in Edinburg, as did many other enrollees from Camp Roosevelt. He was instrumental in getting the Camp Roosevelt Recreation Area built and annually organizes an alumni reunion there.

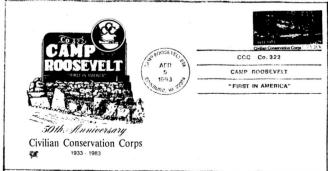

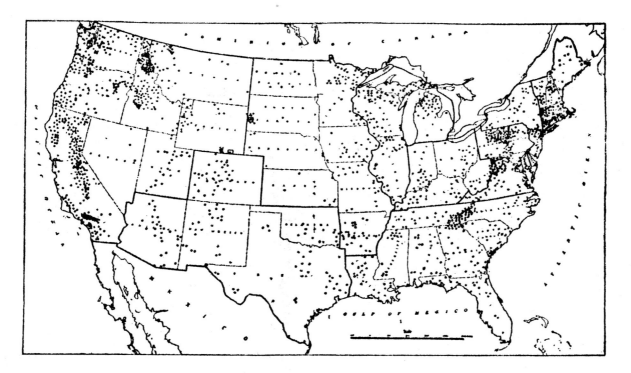

Camps in 1933 were spread throughout the United States. By 1942 more than 4,000 had been established.

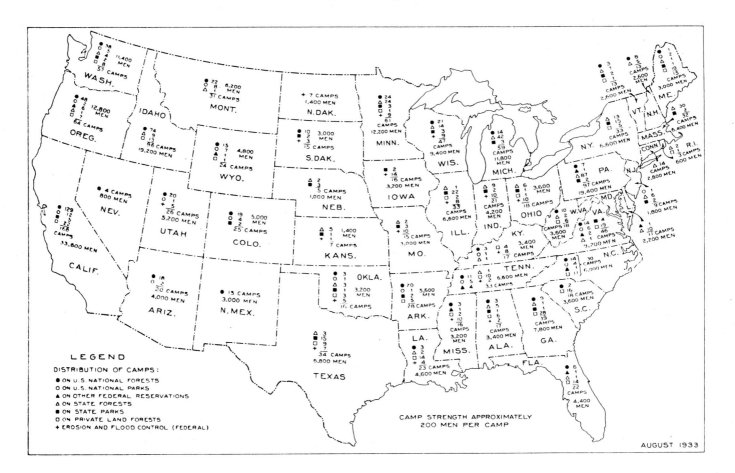

President Roosevelt and
Director Robert Fechner at
Big Meadows.

ARK, VIRGINI

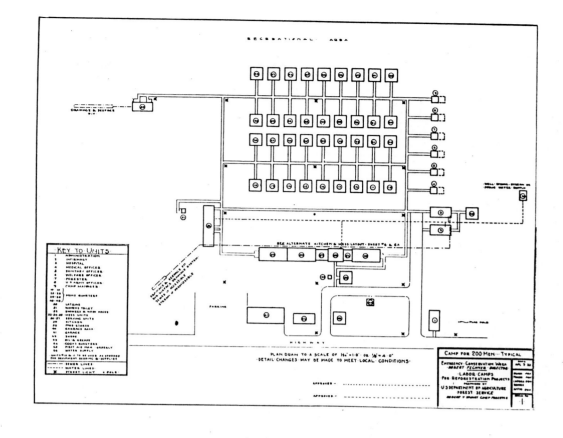

Typical CCC Camp layout for 100 men, April 1933.

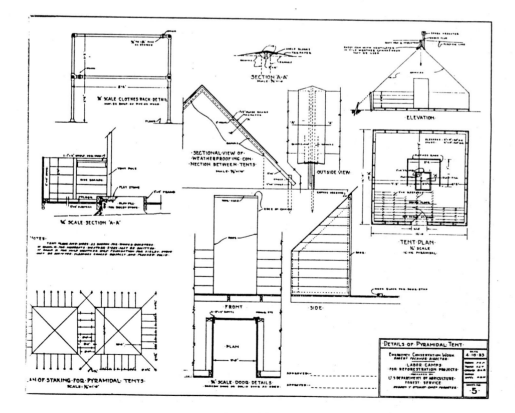

Emergency Conservation Work camps.

CCC boys marching to a gathering at Big Meadows in the Shenandoah National Park, Virginia, 1936. NPS

By the end of 1933, the CCC was an established government organization, beginning to attract attention because of its conservation achievements and its contribution to the depletion of the ranks of unemployed youths.

There were four distinct groups of enrollees. Most numerous were the 250,000 "boys" or Juniors between the ages of 18 and 25. Then there were 25,000 war veterans in their own camps, 25,000 L.E.M. serving as project leaders in the Junior camps, and 10,000 Indians and 5,000 other residents of Alaska, Hawaii, Puerto Rico, and the Virgin Islands.

The Junior enrollee had to be single and from a family on relief. He had to pass a physical examination and live in a camp for a minimum of six months. He could re-enlist, if his work was satisfactory, for six-month hitches up to a maximum of two years. There were no age or marital restrictions on other enrollees. The territorial workers lived at home. Their camps were administered by either the U.S. Forest Service or the Office of Indian Affairs.

The CCC always bore the stigma of being a "relief" organization and never became a permanent agency on a par with others. When it authorized the Corps in 1933, Congress fixed its life at two years, and thereafter gave it periodic extensions. In 1935, the President wanted to increase the enrollment to 600,000 and the age limit for Juniors was raised to 28. Due to problems within several government agencies, the President's enrollment figures were not met.

The great Midwestern drought brought about an increase in CCC enrollment in 1934. Roosevelt called for an increase of 50,000 Juniors and 5,000 veterans in mid-1934, to be recruited from urban centers within the affected areas and placed in camps to help combat the drought.

In September 1935, enrollment peaked at 502,000, organized into 2,514 camps in every state and several territories.

Thereafter, enrollment gradually decreased, dropping below 400,000 in 1937. On April 5 of that year, the President proposed to Congress that the Corps be made a permanent agency. The Senate approved but the House did not, and the Corps was extended only to 1940. It never had another chance to become permanent. The 1937 act greatly increased the authority of the Director, added to the education and training opportunities, changed the age limits for Juniors from 17 to 23 years, dropped the relief requirement for enrollment, and set a manpower maximum of 315,000 in all categories.

From 1933 to 1938, more than 2 million men parti-

Certificate of Discharge
from
Civilian Conservation Corps

TO ALL WHOM IT MAY CONCERN:

THIS IS TO CERTIFY THAT * Darius M. Blake, CCS-193053 A MEMBER OF THE CIVILIAN CONSERVATION CORPS, WHO WAS ENROLLED April 16, 1936 AT Camp F-19, Minnehaha Springs, W.Va. IS HEREBY/DISCHARGED THEREFROM, BY REASON OF ** "Expiration of term of enrollment." S.C. 71, Co. 1580, CCC, dated 9/30/36

SAID Darius M. Blake WAS BORN IN Cranberry, IN THE STATE OF West Virginia WHEN ENROLLED HE WAS 19 YEARS OF AGE AND BY OCCUPATION A Common Labor HE HAD Blue EYES, Light Brown HAIR, Fair COMPLEXION, AND WAS 5 FEET 11 INCHES IN HEIGHT HIS COLOR WAS White

GIVEN UNDER MY HAND AT Camp F-19, Minnehaha Springs, W. Va. THIS 30th DAY OF September ONE THOUSAND NINE HUNDRED AND Thirty-Six

HENRY F. CLICK, 1st Lt. Inf-Res, 398th Inf.
(Name)   (Title)
Commanding.

C.C.C. Form No. 2
April 5, 1933
* Insert name, as "John J. Doe".
** Give reason for discharge.   3—10171

This is the piece of paper that each of the CCC boys started looking for on his first day in service. This particular one shows that Darious M. Blake of Richwood served his time, coming out some 57 years ago.

cipated in the program. During this period the Corps, started strictly for unemployment relief and conservation, evolved into a multi-purpose educational and service organization.

Although the program was praised for its good work, it was racked by internal and external conflicts. Selection policies were changed over the protest of Director Fechner, and his authority was reduced at the instigation of Harry Hopkins, director of the WPA and one of Roosevelt's closest advisors.

Financing was a constant hassle, and the number of enrollees and camps kept going up and down at the whim of the executive department and the appropriations from Congress.

Fechner was a capable administrator but had to fight constantly to assert his authority. Intragovernmental rivalries were a headache for him, and were never completely resolved. Fechner enjoyed visiting the camps around the country. He did not like to sit in his office in Washington.

Everyone had different ideas about how the CCC should be run. Should it be purely a relief organization, or be open to any able-bodied youth? Should it be more work-oriented or more educational-oriented? What projects should it undertake? It is a credit to Fechner and his staff that the organization continued to expand and improve into 1939.

In 1939, the Corps' life was extended to June 30, 1943. It was another of the periodic extensions that hindered long-range planning. At the end of each period of life, work projects were held up until another extension was approved by Congress. Each extension showed, however, that the concept was accepted and the work performed was worth the expense.

By the mid-1930s, the Corps was an established part of life for thousands of people and families throughout the country. The prospect of a closure of a camp brought rigorous protests by the local populace. Most Congressmen supported the camps in their areas and many campaigned for more because of the boost a camp meant for the local economy. Farm products, fuel, lumber, hardware, and other camp items were purchased locally as much as possible. Enrollees spent part of their money in town on weekends. The Corps helped the national economy as well. The three million men enrolled through the years had to be clothed and fed and supplied with tools, machines, and materials, including trucks, cars, trailers, heavy equipment, furniture and office supplies.

In 1933 alone, contracts were let for 500,000 pairs of shoes, 2,500,000 yards of denim, 700,000 pairs of trousers, 1,000,000 towels, 300 cars and 3,000 trucks.

From 12 million to 15 million people directly benefited from the enrollees' monthly allotment checks. More than $700 million was sent to families. The entire cost of the Corps was almost $3 billion in nine years.

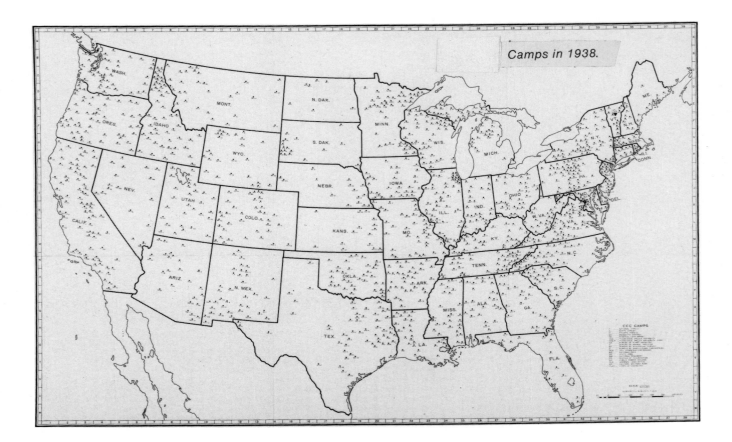

Camps in 1938.

LIBBY & SON.
SPOKANE, WASH.
6498.
C.C.C. Co. 557
CAMP-F-136.

CAMPS

Co. 557, Camp F-136, Enarille, Idaho, 1935.
EASTERN WASHINGTON HISTORICAL SOCIETY

Many different government agencies had responsibilities for CCC camps. The Agriculture Department, through the U.S. Forest Service and Soil Conservation Service (recently transferred from the Interior Department), operated approximately two-thirds of the camps. The Interior Department operated the other third. Through the years, more than 4,000 permanent and side or spike (temporary) camps were built. They were in every state, plus Alaska. Projects were also instituted in Hawaii, Puerto Rico, and the Virgin Islands, but most of the enrollees in these territories lived at home.

Some of the camps were in or close to urban areas; others were in remote regions of the West and Alaska. For the most part, they were an economic boom to the depressed regions where they were located.

A camp designation depended on the agency sponsoring it. Each camp had a number assigned to it, such as NPS (National Park Service) -1 (for first camp). The table below shows in order the letter designation of the camp, land ownership, supervising agency, government department.

A—Agriculture (Bureau of Animal Industry); U.S.F.S. & Bureau of Animal Husbandry; Agriculture.

Army—Military reservations; U.S. Army; War.

BF—Federal Game Refuge (Biological Survey); Bureau of Biol. Survey; Agriculture.

C of E—State Land (Corps of Engineers); U.S. Army; War.

D—Private Land (Drainage); Bureau of Ag. Engineering; Agriculture.

DG—Public Domain; Div. of Grazing; Interior.

F—National Forests; U.S. Forest Service; Agriculture.

L—State and Federal Land (Levee); U.S.F.S. & State; Agriculture.

MC—Private Land (Mosquito Control); U.S.F.S. & State; Agriculture.

MP—Military Park; National Park Ser.; Interior.

NA—National Arboretum (Bureau of Plant Ind.); U.S.F.S.; Agriculture.

Navy—Naval Mil. Res.; U.S.F.S. & U.S. Navy (except Navy-1-Va., by N.P.S. & Navy); Agriculture.

NHP—National Historical Park; National Park Ser.; Interior.

P—Private Forest; U.S. Forest Service & State; Agriculture.

PE—Private Land Erosion; U.S. Forest Service & State; Agriculture.

S—State Forest; U.S. Forest Service & State; Agriculture.

SCS—Private Land; Soil Conservation Service; Agriculture.

SP—State Park; State Park Division of National Park Service & State; Interior.

TVA—Tennessee Valley Authority; U.S. Forest Service & Tennessee Valley Authority; Agriculture.

TVA-P—Tennessee Valley Authority; State Park Division of National Park Service & Tennessee Valley Authority; Interior.

The War Department administered the camps. The department was divided into these nine corps areas:

FIRST—Maine, New Hampshire, Vermont, Massachusetts, Rhode Island, and Connecticut with headquarters at Boston.

SECOND—New Jersey, Delaware, and New York, with headquarters at Governors Island, New York.

Co. 1387, Camp Nira, Shenandoah National Park.
SNP

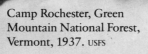

Camp Rochester, Green
Mountain National Forest,
Vermont, 1937. USFS

Cumberland Falls State Park Camp in Whitley County,
Kentucky, 1934. USFS

THIRD—Pennsylvania, Maryland, Virginia, and the District of Columbia, with headquarters at Baltimore.

FOURTH—North Carolina, South Carolina, Georgia, Alabama, Tennessee, Mississippi, and Louisiana, with headquarters at Atlanta.

FIFTH—Ohio, West Virginia, Indiana, and Kentucky, with headquarters at Columbus.

SIXTH—Illinois, Michigan, and Wisconsin, with headquarters at Chicago.

SEVENTH—Kansas, Arkansas, Iowa, Nebraska, North Dakota, South Dakota, Minnesota, and Missouri, with headquarters at Omaha.

EIGHTH—Texas, Oklahoma, Colorado, New Mexico, Arizona, and Wyoming (less Yellowstone National Park), with headquarters at Houston.

NINTH—Washington, Oregon, Idaho, Montana, Utah, Nevada, California, and Yellowstone National Park, with headquarters at San Francisco.

The Forest Service consisted of 10 regions covering all states plus Alaska and Puerto Rico. The National Park Service had three regions in the United States.

Each Camp consisted of a company, and its number usually indicated the Army Corps area in which the company was formed. This numbering system for camps and companies changed considerably over the years. Many of the camps acquired local names such as the Nine Mile Camp, Montana; Sunset Camp, Washington; and Camp Rochester, Vermont.

The National Park Service operated a camp near Mt. McKinley National Park in Alaska and ran other CCC operations in Alaska and Hawaii.

Each company had a company commander, who was either a regular army or reserve officer, plus a junior officer, camp doctor, and educational adviser. The project superintendent, usually employed by the technical service the camp was under, was in charge of all work projects away from camp and had eight to ten foremen under him. The foremen were usually "Local Experienced Men," known as L.E.M.

Each camp was composed of one company of approximately 200 men. The enrollees were eligible to become "rated" men to help with the camp administration, usually a senior leader, mess steward, storekeeper, and two cooks. Assistant leaders were the company clerk, assistant educational adviser, and three second cooks. These men were picked from the company roster

Camp F-1, on the Catahoula unit of the Kisatchie National Forest, Louisiana, 1934. USFS

and were paid $45 and $36 a month, depending on the rating, compared to $30 per month for an enrollee.

The average camp had 24 buildings, including kitchen and mess hall, recreational building, school building, infirmary, barracks for the enrollees, and quarters for the officers and enlisted personnel. Each camp was a city in itself. It had food, health, educational, religious, and entertainment facilities along with facilities for blacksmithing, plumbing, and automotive repair.

In the early days, most camps began as collections of army pyramid or bell tents housing four to six men each. These served until permanent buildings could be erected, at times by the enrollees themselves. Meals often were served outdoors until the mess hall could be built. The sturdy but unpretentious barracks buildings accommodated 40 to 50 men each.

By 1936, camps were being built of portable precut buildings so that buildings could be moved after work was finished in an area. A standard design was adopted and each new camp consisted of four barracks, a mess hall, bath houses, a latrine, school building, and 12 other buildings to house army personnel and various support services.

With more than 4,000 camps built in the CCC's nine-year history, every conceivable type of site was built on. Camps sprouted among the towering redwoods of California, in logged or burned-over areas in the Northwest, in desert areas of the Southwest, in the wind-swept flatlands of the Dakotas, Nebraska, and Kansas, on lake shores in Minnesota and Wisconsin, near urban areas of the East, in timbered areas of the South, in swamplands in Louisiana, at sea level and on mountainsides. In one year California had 98 camps, while Delaware and Rhode Island had four each and the District of Columbia two.

A permanent camp sometimes had several side or spike camps set up for particular projects. These were usually tent camps.

Many of the camps in the West were populated by enrollees from the East, many of whom had not been beyond the borders of their country or state before. For them, the CCC was a great adventure.

Of the over 4,000 camps built in the United States very little evidence is left of them today. One camp in eastern West Virginia is now used as a national youth science camp site. The Rabideau Historic Site on the Blackduck Ranger District of the Chippewa National Forest in northern Minnesota is a preserved CCC camp completed in 1935. It housed Company 708 until 1941 and then was used for years as a summer camp of the University of Illinois. Seventeen buildings remaining at the site are now on the National Register of Historic Places.

1ST LT. MARTIN COLE'S CCC EXPERIENCE

Martin Cole was a typical unemployed man in 1934 but held a reserve Second Lieutenant's commission in the U.S. Army. Regular Army personnel in charge of CCC camps were being replaced by reserve officers, so Cole got a job in 1934 from New Orleans. Five years of intermittent duty took him to various camps in the Fourth Corps area including Co. 1401 (F-2) Ocala, Fl., Co. 452 (P-60) Woodbine, Ga., Co. 1488 (I-57) Laplace, La., Co. 4423 (F-1) Dude, Ms., Co. 4416 (SCS-11) Harrisonburg, La., Co. 428 (F-14) Balsam Grove, N.C., later the same company at John Rock, N.C., Co. 411 (NP-5) Smokemont, N.C., Co. 5405 (F-4) Leesville, La. and Co. 1494 Grangerville, La. Five of these camps were under his command.

He spent World War Two with the U.S. Army Corps of Engineers and then for 19 years was associated with the California Parks and Recreation Department. He is now retired and lives in Whittier, Calif.

1st Lt. Martin Cole.

Lt. Cole and Co. 452 basketball team.

Camp Satilla Bluff, Co. 452 (P-60) Woodbine, Ga.

Officers at camp F-28 John Rock near Brevard, N.C. Left to right: Carter Whittaker, educational advisor; Lt. Tom Shackleford, junior officer; Lt. Martin Cole, camp commander; and Lt. Morris Kanner, camp doctor.

Officers at F-14 Balsam Grove, NC camp, 1937. Standing: 1st Lt. John Peacock and 2nd Lt. Melvin Levy. Kneeling: Carter Whittaker and 1st Lt. Cole.

Barracks No 4, John Rock camp.

Mess Hall, P-60 camp Woodbine, Ga.

THE CASE OF THE MISSING MOP HEAD

The CCC District Headquarters considered Captain Bumbelford a superior officer. Yet never once during the Captain's tours of duty as a camp commander were complimentary gestures extended toward him. It does seem strange since General Julius Caeser Pinchbeck, District Commander, found a few opportunities to require the Captain to explain by endorsement why he failed to accomplish such and such.

In order to maintain a highly organized and efficient daily routine, as set forth in the "book," it was generally necessary for the Captain to complete two days' work in one. He seldom turned to his humble G.I. steel cot before midnight.

Somehow, the Captain managed to maintain an undisturbed equanimity. That is, he did, until one day he received an official red-bordered letter, with "Subject: Missing Mop Head." What literally lifted the Captain from his chair was a charge his property records failed to account for (1) mop head!

Mop heads are issued in two colors—green and red. Other than the color, all are identical. However, the Army classifies the green ones as "expendable," the red ones as "non-expendable." An officer is not accountable for expendable property. After a green mop head is worn out, it is carted away to the trash. Not so with a red one. Once it becomes unservicable, it must be stored, and notated on an I&I Report. Later it is turned into the District Quartermaster, who issues a credit memorandum receipt. Captain Bumbleford was charged with being short a red mop head—value twelve cents.

A thorough search of the company files failed to uncover information that would reveal when or how the Captain acquired the red mop head. Even though the Captain could not recall having seen this article, military discipline had taught him that a General can never be wrong. Therefore he assumed that somewhere about his camp could be found the missing mop head. A shakedown inspection failed to locate it.

Bumbleford next held a company meeting. Someone suggested that a search be made of the stone quarry.

The Captain's face brightened. He remembered that each day a couple extra duty boys emptied G.I. cans of trash into the abandoned pit.

"By Jove," he thundered. "The very place to look." And then his jaw dropped, as he was reminded by half a dozen enrollees that the quarry was half full of water.

The water must be drained. Then a search could be made through two year's sodden debris for a lone non-expendable mop head. But for the Captain, it was a matter-of-fact responsibility of performing another quite insurmountable task.

Captain Bumbleford managed to secure from the Forest Service two motor-driven pumps. Day after day, night after night, the pumps continued their uninterrupted pumping. When the water reached the ankle deep stage, a detail of enrollees wearing boots began sifting huge piles of soggy rubbish. Late in the afternoon, the leader-in-charge reported to Captain Bumbleford.

"Well," exclaimed the Captain, searching the lad's expressionless face for a clue. "Did you find the mop head?"

"No, sir," replied the enrollee, "but, sir, we've found our other Army truck—you know the one that was lost some time ago? It was at the bottom of the quarry, covered with mud."

"Dang it," cried the officer, "didn't I want you to find the mop head? We weren't looking for an Army truck—were we? Somebody tell me what are we going to do now?"

At that moment, by coincidence, the District Commander was framing in his mind a tentative answer to Bumbleford's perplexing question. At Headquarters General Pinchbeck was meeting with his staff. "Gentlemen," began the General, "a mop head has been lost. It must be found. Now, tomorrow, each of you in your official automobiles will form a convoy, I, of course leading. We will drive to Captain Bumbleford's camp. Once there, it is expected that the missing mop will be located."

Captain Bumbleford had just finished a late lunch, when his orderly informed him of the arrival of a convoy. Before the Captain had time to straighten his tie, the delegation was upon him. "How do you do, Captain," exclaimed the General pumping the Captain's hand. "So glad to see you. You know these gentlemen, don't you?"

"We are here," went on the General, "on important business, Captain. Let's see where would anyone most likely find a mop? Why in the kitchen of course. Lead the way, Captain. I must say your camp is looking mighty fine. Well here's the Mess Hall."

An awkward moment followed as the General's ▶

staff, and the Captain awaited the General's first move. It came immediately. The General's eyes gazed beyond the stove to the mop rack. With the look of a tiger zeroing on its prey, General Pinchbeck sprang toward the mop rack where hung a mop with a green head.

He yanked the mop off the rack. Spinning about, and thrusting it under the Captain's nose, he screamed, "What the hell kind of officer are you, anyway? You make me spend a hundred dollars of the government's money to come here and find a missing mop head. You could have just as well gotten off your dead end, and found it yourself. Bumbleford, you're a discredit to the service. Shut up. Don't interrupt! I'll do the talk-ing, do you understand? Now get this, Bumbleford, if you want to stay on CCC duty, you're going to have to snap out of it! But I'm going to be lenient this time. That's my biggest fault, I am too big hearted with you Reserve Officers. I am going to give you one more chance. And if you understand English, you will realize that hereafter it's entirely up to you. I will have the Quartermaster issue you a credit memo for the mop head. Good day sir. Come, gentlemen let us be going."

Said one Second Lieutenant to another, in the last car of the convoy as it left the camp, "Right funny about the old man becoming color blind in his old age, and believing green is red."   —MARTIN COLE

A friendly critique after inspection at the John Rock camp. Lt. Cole, commanding officer, talks to camp personnel.

Co. 428 F-28 John Rock camp, Brevard, NC, where Cole wrote his Mop Head story.

BALSAM BREEZE

VOLUME 2   COMPANY 428, CCC CAMP N. C. F-14, BALSAM GROVE, N. C OCTOBER 1937   NUMBER 7

CAMP F-14 TO LOSE 30 ENROLLEES OCT. 1

LEWIS MORRIS SAVES LIFE

Mr. O. A. Jones, 47, of Jackson, N. C., owes his life to Lewis Morris, NC F-14 enrollee who pulled him from the Davidson River, and brought him back to life after he was apparently drowned.

Jones was driving a heavy motor grader machine along the Davidson River road, when it left the highway and plunged down a 20 foot embankment into the river where he was submerged and entangled in the wrecked cab of the machine.

A motorist from Mississippi who witnessed the accident, quickly secured the aid of local mountaineers, and Lewis Morris, who is stationed at the Pisgah Forest picnic grounds. Together they rescued Jones, after he had spent at least eight or ten minutes submerged.

Enrollee Morris immdiately started administering artificial respiration and it was nearly a half hour later before the unconscious man revealed signs of life. An ambulance summoned from the Lyday hospital of Brevard, soon thereafter arrived on the scene and Mr. Jones was sent to that institution where he was treated for shock.

Had not Lewis Morris applied himsel to the study of First Aid, that is offered to all CCC enrollees, there is very little doubt as to what the outcome of this incident might have been.

F-14 Wins Sub-District Softball

Overcoming a lead of 9 to 4, F-14 softball players rallied in the seventh inning to win over Co. 438, SCS F-1, in the play-off September 12, for the Sub-District championship. The final score was 10-9. Neither team previous to that day had been defeated.

F-14 got off with a bad start, and the outcome looked dark for our boys until the last of the seventh inning, when Martin led off with the first run. From that minute on everyone realized that F-14 had the game in the bag.

F-14 lineup consisted of King, 1b; Nixon, 2b; Suggart, ss; Sisk, 3b; Trimm, lf; Fuller, rf; Owens, c; Brown, sf; Gurley, cf; and Bridges, p. Substitutes were Bingham Turner and Martin. On the following night these players were treated to the movie, "Souls at Sea", at the expense of the Company Fund.

LIEUT. COLE NEW SKIPPER

1st. Lt. Martin G. Cole, who hails from New Orleans, assumed command of Company 428, on September 1st. relieving Captain Francis S. Davenport, upon that officer's completion of the customary six months tour of duty. Lieutenant Cole has had sufficient experience with the CCC to whip this organization into a crack outfit, and one of his primary aims is to make our company an outstanding example within District "B".

By way of background, Lieutenant Cole, originally was an Illinois "Corn 'Husker end there attended Illinois State Normal University. Thereafter he served as an instructor at the Pacific Military Academy, Hollywood, Calif., then spent a year with the Department of Interior, surveying military roads in Alaska, this followed by a position as one on the Engineering Staff of a hard rock mine in California, from whence he later journed to New Orleans to take up further engineering work. Lieutenant Cole states that Co. 428, is his eighth CCC Camp. He was initiated into the CCC, back in 1934, and cut his military wisdom teeth at Company 1401, Ocala, Florida. Thereafter he gained additional experience in camps located in Georgia, Louisiana, Mississippi and North Carolina.

Led by Leader Oscar Harbin, veteran member of Company 428, approximately 30 men who have been here from two to three years or who are over age, will be gone by October 1st. Some will go back to the farms, others to factories; in North Carolina. South Carolina and Georgia, and many, no doubt, will remain indefinitely in Transylvania county lured by tinkling wedding bells.

These years have been happy ones for the fellows leaving. Only 'yesterday it seems they arrived, rookies raw and skinny. The months sped by and they grew mentally, physically and morally. Many were promoted and held positions of responsibility and service. They learned much from those in authority. At first all felt lost and helpless, the camp being so isolated, but soon each learned to love the quiet beauty of the Pisgahs with its endless unbroken forests and mountain chains that disappeared on distant horizons. Deer and other abundant wildlife brought a closeness to nature that none had ever experienced.

Now the old guard of Company 428 is being disbanded. Many have already gone. No company, back from battle, ever separated with more regret. Their enemy has been depression and forest fire and the enemies of the wild creatures of the woods. They return to fight again, to fight the sorrow of leaving pals and camp where they spent so many happy months, to fight for a place in the working world, alone but unafraid.

When they first heard that October 1st. was really to be the last day, many began to drift away in two and threes as work became available. However, most of them are staying until the last, hopeful that the efforts for securing employment, made by the Commanding Officer, together with the Project Superintendent, will prove successful in their behalf. Both Lt. Cole and Mr. Maneval are cooperating with the National CCC Employment program, hundreds of letters were sent from this camp to prospective employers requesting them to consider CCC boys who have learned tolerance and understanding.

Old F-14 is gone. A new era begins. It will always be a bright and pleasant spot in their memories. It is hoped those that stay will take full advantage of all that the camp has to offer and will carry on in the footsteps of the old men to make a better company.

THIS PAPER PRINTED BY THE PRINTING CLASS OF COMPANY 428 AT THE F-14 PRINT SHOP

Officers looking over a new group of enrollees.

Print shop.

Woodworking shop.

Cooks.

Wise River camp in Montana, 1933. MONTANA HISTORICAL
SOCIETY

Local enrollees from the Butte, Montana area at the Wise
River camp in 1933, shown with their L.E.M.'s.
MONTANA HISTORICAL SOCIETY

A camp in the Whitman National Forest, Washington,
1935.

Located at Uncioi, Tennessee, this camp was named for
U.S. Secretary of State Cordell Hull and was one of the
first four in the state, 1933. NA

Portable bunk house at a spike camp in the Siskiyou National Forest in Oregon. USFS

A camp in the desert of Arizona, 1936. NA

Camp warehouse in the Sumter National Forest, South Carolina, 1935.
USFS

Portage River camp in the La Croix Ranger District, Superior National Forest in Minnesota, 1940. USFS

Camp Alvon in the Monongahela National Forest, West Virginia. USFS

Gegoka Camp on the shore of McDougal Lake in the Superior National Forest, Minnesota, 1940. Camps were established throughout the lake areas of Minnesota and Wisconsin. USFS

Camp F-64-A in the Coronado National Forest, Arizona, 1941. USFS

A side camp in the woods of Upper Michigan. The buildings to the left are for office personnel and tool storage. NA

A CCC camp in Beltsville, Maryland, looking toward the company headquarters, 1936. USFS

Co. 2920, F-1, Camp Sullivan, Sullivan Lake, Washington, 1935. EASTERN WASHINGTON HISTORICAL SOCIETY

Stanley Lake spike camp in the Sawtooth National Forest, Idaho, 1937. The rugged scenery must have been a thrill for enrollees, especially those from the Midwest or East. USFS

Co. 963, F-47 Lolo National Forest, 1935. UNIVERSITY OF MONTANA ARCHIVES

MORNING WORK CALL, VCCC CO. 1779, BURR O
FORMATION BEFORE LEAVING

Views of Veteran Camp 179, Burr
Oak, Kansas. KANSAS HISTORICAL SOCIETY

HOSPITAL, VCCC CO. 1779, BURR OAK, KS.

ARMY DRIVERS, VCCC CO. 1779, BURR OAK, KS.
BRADLEY (LEFT), SINCLAIR (RIGHT)

HOSPITAL STAFF, VCCC CO. 1779
BURR OAK, KS. LEFT TO RIGHT
HUTCHESON, RICHMOND, HARRELL

Jornada Camp in Cibola National Forest, New Mexico in 1934. USFS

A National Park Service camp at Mammoth Hot Springs, Yellowstone National Park, Wyoming, 1934. NPS

A spike camp in the tall timber on Eagle Creek Trail in Oregon, 1935. USFS

Soapstone Camp, F-6 on the Wasatch National Forest, Utah, 1934. USFS

Educational buildings at a typical CCC camp. NA

Camp NP-4 at No Name Creek in Glacier National Park, Montana, 1934. This must have been an ideal location for a summer spike camp. MONTANA HISTORICAL SOCIETY

Camp at St. Croix, Virgin Islands. NA

Birch Creek Camp, Beaverhead National Forest, Montana, 1936. Part of this camp is still in use for outdoor education classes from Western Montana College.
MONTANA HISTORICAL SOCIETY

Co. 1999, Camp Needmore on the Custer National Forest near Ekalaka, Montana, 1935. The camp is still in use for 4-H clubs and the Ekalaka community.
MONTANA HISTORICAL SOCIETY

Camp P-210, Borill, Idaho.
USFS

A spike camp east of Alberton, Montana, on the Lolo National Forest. USFS

Bungalow camp in the Clearwater National Forest, Idaho, 1939. USFS

Camp F-44 near Clarkia, Idaho. USFS

Barracks and water tower at Camp Hoffman, a state forest camp in North Carolina, 1935. USFS

Spruce Hill Side Camp in the White Mountain National Forest, New Hampshire, 1935. USFS

Lawton Camp on Jackson Creek, Apache National Forest, Arizona. NA

Local carpenters repairing the walls of the Wildwood Camp barracks in the White Mountain National Forest, New Hampshire, 1939. USFS

Nelsonville Camp in the Wayne National Forest of southeastern Ohio, 1940. USFS

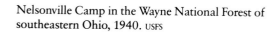

First snow of the season at the Park Side Camp in the Holy Cross National Forest, Colorado, October 1934. USFS

Rudy Forest Service camp on the Beaverhead National Forest, Montana, 1933. USFS

Initial tent camp at Atlantic, Cass County, Iowa, 1934. USFS

Camp in the Mt. Hood National Forest, Oregon, 1936. USFS

NINE MILE CCC CAMP, ALBERTON, MONTANA

The Nine Mile Camp, located in the Nine Mile Valley near Alberton, Montana, in the Lolo National Forest, was the largest CCC camp in the country, housing three companies of 200 men each. They helped build the historic Remount Station at the Nine Mile Ranger District. USFS

Headquarters building at the Nine Mile Camp, 1933.

Chimney and foundation remains at the Nine Mile Camp. The camp area is now a Forest Service historic site along with the Remount Station and present ranger station.

Enrollees fall in for a work detail at the Shavers Fork
Spike Camp near Elkins, West Virginia, 1933. NA

CAMP LIFE

*C*amp life was far different from anything the enrollees had experienced. Many were away from home for the first time and were holding their first steady jobs. To urban youths the sudden transfer to a remote wilderness camp was a real cultural shock. In addition, camp life was regimented; the enrollees had to follow a standard daily routine. No longer would he roam the streets of his hometown or the backwoods of his farm, or "ride the rails" in search of work. On the other hand, while the pay of a dollar a day was hardly lavish, he did have some income for himself and was earning money for the family back home.

The candidate first was interviewed by the local selecting agency to determine his capacity to benefit from the CCC program. (In the early years, there were five applicants for every opening.) He then had to pass a physical examination, and after that he took the oath of enrollment. Once officially in the CCC, he was sent to an Army base for a short period of time for conditioning before going to his assigned camp. The first recruits in the spring and summer of 1933 sometimes had to wait until a campsite was ready, or help build the camp. As more camps were erected the enrollees spent less time on construction. In 1937, precut portable camps came into use, speeding construction considerably.

Most of the boys enrolling in the early days were underweight and undernourished. They gained an average of 11¼ pounds in their first three to four months in the CCC.

Health and safety were of primary importance. The Army was in charge of health facilities, and each camp had the services of either a medical reserve officer or a contract physician from the area. All enrollees received inoculations against typhoid fever and smallpox. Each camp had an infirmary; illness or potential illness was treated quickly to prevent the spread of disease and to get an enrollee back to work.

The War Department set down some personal hygiene standards that each enrollee was supposed to follow: He had to bathe at least once a week, clean his teeth daily, keep his hair short, keep his fingernails short and clean, and keep his bedding and clothing clean.

A dentist visited each camp at least every six months; emergency dental work was usually done at the nearest Army center or at the office of a private dentist.

Camp leaders, assistant leaders, technical supervisors, and truck drivers were required to have first aid certificates, and when national defense training came along in 1940, enrollees took first-aid training, too.

Accidents were always a serious problem. About half of the fatal accidents involved vehicles. Other major causes of death were drowning, falls, falling objects, railroad incidents and fire fighting. There were some suicides and some deaths from disease. The rate of fatal accidents was cut over the years from 1.14 per thousand to .90 per thousand due to increased safety training. The overall death rate was 2.25 per thousand.

Base pay was $30 per month and of this, $22 to $25 was sent to the enrollee's family. For veterans and enrollees with no families, most of the pay was put in savings accounts. What the enrollee kept he used for candy, cigarettes, tobacco, toilet articles, movies and dates.

Recruits arriving at the Ft. Hoyle, Maryland, conditioning camp in 1933 for a two-week training period. NA

Enrollees get physicals and shots before starting work. NA

The typical daily routine meant Reveille at 6 A.M. and breakfast at 6:30. After this came sick call and policing of the campsite. At 7:15, trucks were loaded with men and tools to start the day's work project. The boys worked under experienced foremen and received on-the-job training. Thirty minutes was allotted to the lunch break, and at 4 P.M., the trucks headed back to camp. The retreat ceremony, involving flag lowering, inspection and announcements came at 5 P.M. Dinner followed, and from then until lights out at 10 P.M., the enrollee was free to read, write letters, attend a class, or shoot the bull with friends.

Beer was available at some canteens but hard liquor was forbidden. Drunkenness could be grounds for dismissal from the Corps.

No standard leave time was ever adopted. Leave time was flexible, depending on how far the enrollee was from public transportation facilities. He could make two trips home during the six-month enrollment period unless home was thousands of miles away. He could leave camp on weekends.

Religious services were conducted at most camps, either by Army chaplains or by civilian religious leaders who lived in the area. Enrollees were welcome in community churches.

Moral standards varied and did not seem to be affected by the camp experience. Gambling, drinking, and sexual activities were problems, but the regimented life tended to reduce them. If an enrollee could not cope with the program, he usually deserted or was given a discharge.

The camps held dances, plays, and musical programs. Sports activity was encouraged. Leagues were formed amongst camps in an area for many indoor and outdoor sports. Money was collected from individuals and camp fundraising activities to buy uniforms and equipment. Many different arts and crafts were taught in the evenings and on weekends.

Life in a camp involved close association with 200 other men of diverse backgrounds. It included good meals, hard work, a good sleep every night and a regular schedule. It had a profound effect on the millions of men who experienced it. Their health and attitudes improved. The country, too, benefited, not only from the men's conservation work, but also from their strengthened outlook on life and living.

Raising the flag at a camp in the Nevada National Forest, Nevada, 1940. USFS

An army-style formation at Kyle Canyon Camp, Nevada, in June 1940. Reveille and retreat were held every day at camps throughout the country. USFS

Flag ceremony at the Middletown Spike Camp, Lake County, California, 1939. CALIFORNIA STATE LIBRARY

Supervisory personnel, army, navy and civilian at a camp in the St. Maries, Idaho, district, 1933.
EASTERN WASHINGTON
HISTORICAL SOCIETY

MEDICAL FACILITIES

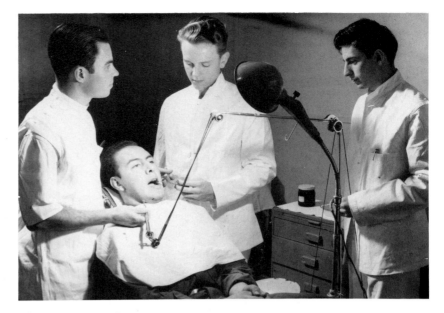

Two assistants—one of them operating the foot engine that powered drills and brushes—work with Dr. H.B. Palmer of Santa Fe, New Mexico, a CCC dentist who had 12 camps on his circuit in 1940. NA

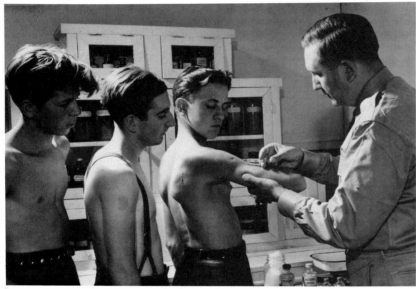

CCC enrollees received excellent medical care. It was cheaper to prevent sickness than to treat it. Here a camp doctor is giving an examination at Gegoka Camp, Superior National Forest, Minnesota, 1940. NA

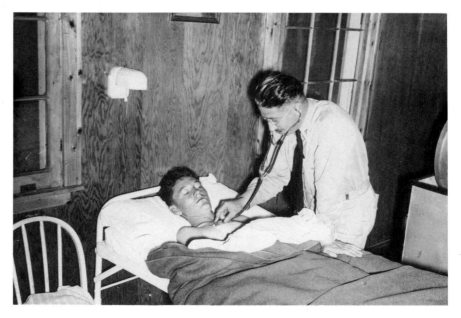

USFS

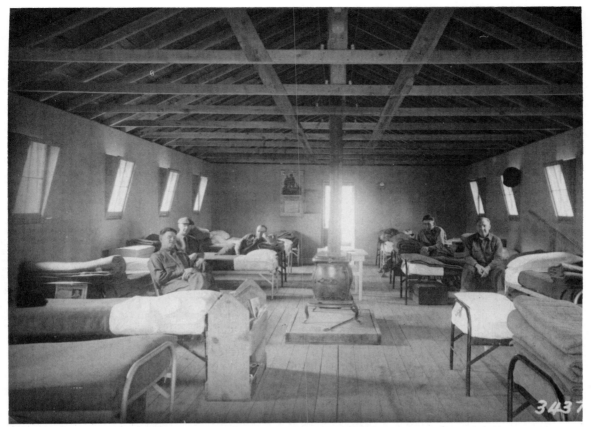

Enrollees relax in their barracks at Camp F-20, Park Creek, Black Hills National Forest, South Dakota, 1937. USFS

Morning inspection of a barracks at Camp F-1, Nebraska National Forest, near Halsey, Nebraska, 1940. This routine inspection was to insure good health and neatness of the enrollee. USFS

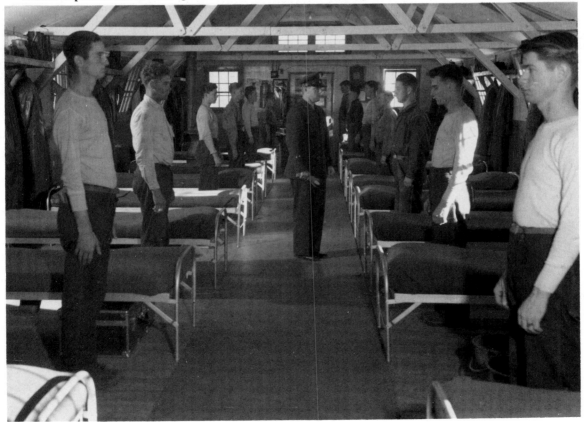

SUPPLIES

Enrollees get spruce-green uniforms and other new clothes at a reception center in New Cumberland, Pennsylvania, 1941. NA

A supply room at Camp Sun Valley No. 1383, Sunbury, Pennsylvania, 1941. USFS

Candy, tobacco, cigarettes and toilet articles are sold at the canteen of Company 3350, Camp Orogrande, New Mexico, 1940. NA

SPORTS AND RELIGION

Baseball was the major summer sport at camps throughout the country. This team was from Company 446, D-92, Brunswick, Georgia. NA

Mass at Camp Roosevelt, Virginia, 1940. NA

A church service on the shore of Jackson Lake, Jackson Hole, Wyoming, 1933. NA

MUSICAL ACTIVITIES

Hillbilly band at the Mormon Creek Camp, Hiawatha National Forest, Michigan, 1939. USFS

The orchestra of Company 2595 at Petersburg, West Virginia. NA

The drum corps of Camp Santa Fe, SP-1, New Mexico, 1940. The corps participated in parades in nearby towns. NA

Camp orchestra, Camp Triangle, Virginia, 1940. NA

EDUCATION

A CCC writing class. Educational opportunities increased as the CCC grew older. NA

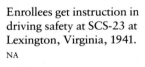

Enrollees get instruction in driving safety at SCS-23 at Lexington, Virginia, 1941. NA

An art class meets at Company 788, SP-27, Lake View, Iowa. NA

Enrollees at Camp SP-1, Hyde State Park, Santa Fe, New Mexico, in the Cooks and Bakers School, prepare biscuits for the camp dinner as part of their assigned work, 1940. NA

Food storage at the Poore Mountain Side Camp of Camp Triangle, Virginia, 1940. NA

An enrollee putting meringue on lemon pies at the Gegoka Camp, Superior National Forest, Minnesota, 1940. USFS

Many enrollees were taught on the job how to cook for large groups. Camp kitchen at the Gegoka Camp, Superior National Forest, Minnesota, 1940. USFS

KP duty at Ft. Slocum, New York, a conditioning camp set up in 1933. NA

Mess hall with Thanksgiving dinner in a Wyoming camp, 1936. WYOMING STATE ARCHIVES

A baker at Camp Roosevelt, Virginia, 1940. NA

Enrollees at Camp SP-1, Hyde State Park, Santa Fe, New Mexico, in the Cooks and Bakers School prepare biscuits for the camp dinner as part of their assigned work, 1940. NA

The kitchen at the Packwood Ranger Station, Columbia National Forest, Washington, 1936. USFS

Learning to cut meat at Camp SP-1, Hyde State Park, Santa Fe, New Mexico, 1940. NA

An outdoor kitchen at a camp near Porter Springs, south of Roosevelt Lake, Tonto National Forest, Arizona, 1939. USFS

Work call line-up and roll call, then a turnover of the men from Army control to Forest Service control for the day. Roll is called by the Senior Leader (standing alone in front of line of boys) with assignments, announcements, etc., made at this time. The truck drivers are stationed by their trucks, Chippewa National Forest, Minnesota, 1940. USFS

Work call, Mormon Creek Camp, Hiawatha National Forest, Michigan, 1939.

Arrivals at West Yellowstone,
Montana, on their way to camps in
Yellowstone National Park, 1934. NPS

Enrollees at the Middletown Spike
Camp of Camp Northwestern,
California Division of Forestry.
CALIFORNIA STATE LIBRARY

Enrollees waiting to board a train at
West Yellowstone, Montana, 1936. NPS

The library and reading room at the Mormon Creek Camp, Hiawatha National Forest, Michigan, 1939. Most camps had libraries. USFS

Library of Gegoka Camp, Superior National Forest, Minnesota, 1940. USFS

Recreation hall at Camp P-60, Chatom, Alabama, 1935. USFS

WRITTEN BY THE C.C.C. FOR THE C.C.C.

HAPPY DAYS EVERY WEEK

SEND HAPPY DAYS HOME

Happy Days

The National Weekly Newspaper for the Civilian Conservation Corps

Vol. 6, No. 5   WASHINGTON, D. C., SATURDAY, JUNE 11, 1938   Five Cents   Matter at D. C. Post Office Entered as Second Class

CORPS WILL BE EXPANDED TO 299,800

CCC Gets More Ratings as Co's. Are Boosted to 200 Men

25,000 EASTERN MEN TO BE SENT WEST

JOINED SEARCH—Part of the small army of CCC men who joined thousands of civilians in a man-hunt for kidnaped James Bailey Cash Jr., whose disappearance from his home started the greatest man-hunt in history of Florida and aroused the nation. Finding of the boy's body, Thursday, brought to a halt activity of searchers who were combing the great wild and swampy country around Princeton, where the child was snatched from his crib.

Acme-News Pictures

C-Men Carry Injured Mountaineer 11 Miles in Eight Weary Hours

Seven enrollees took turns carrying an injured man thru dense woods to camp after his 800-foot slide down the slope of Mt. Stuart, near Co. 983, Leavenworth, Wash.

Led by Douglas Muir and Harold Werner, the crew struggled thru heavy undergrowth and timber for eight hours before the 11-mile trip was completed.

The camp surgeon treated the man for minor back injuries and sent him to Yakima in a truck.

With a party of mountaineers, he was trying to scale the 9700-foot peak when he slipped and fell.

From 56th to 4th

Since last October, when Co. 3760, Poplar Bluff, Mo., was 56th in the affections of Missouri-Kansas district inspectors, the outfit has come far.

Latest achievement is gaining the

Corporation Has a Heart

As a small boy, Howard Jackson used to follow his father about while the latter made his rounds as building custodian of a Pasadena bank.

While young Jackson was enrolled in Co 2923-C, Elsinore, Calif., his father was killed in a motor accident. The bank immediately got in touch with the youth and offered him his father's job.

Jackson took it. Tho he hasn't been in the bank since he was a child, he and the officials both feel he has some experience in the work.

Capt. Leaves CCC After 61 Months of Service

Completing the longest tour of duty of any captain in the Fifth Corps Area, Capt. John P. West leaves the service with fond farewells from his latest command, Co 3527, Morgantown, W Va.

Capt West has served with the CCC since April 27, 1933, for a total of 5 years 1 month and 4 days. He returned to civil life May 31, 1938.

During Capt West's tour as camp commander, one of his camps (P-54) was singled out as the best in the Fifth Corps Area. For this distinction each member of the company was awarded a medal by the Reserve Officers Association. While under his command, Co 3527 always rated excellent. Maj Gen. W. E. Cole, Fifth Corps Area commander, wrote a letter of commendation concerning the improvements made.

Capt West leaves the CCC with a top-ranking record and with the best wishes of his former associates.—ACEA Collins reporting

No Badges Needed by These Cops

"Pull over to the side!" coming from any member of the supervisory personnel or an enrollee driver has an exact connotation at Co. 2584, Beverly, W. Va. It means "This is a pinch."

If you're a truck driver and you break a state driving regulation, any other camp driver has the authority to give you a ticket for it. And he's armed with tickets, too.

After that, you're hauled up before the camp's "justice of the peace."

That's the way Project Supt. L. F. Silberberger has it worked out, and it's getting results. Drivers are rated according to the number of tickets they're presented with, and

32 Ohio Camps Buy Sound Projection Equipment

Each of the 32 camps in the Ohio District have purchased sound motion picture projectors.

Three men—adviser, assistant adviser, and one other enrollee—of each camp are being trained to operate the machines. Films for camp programs will be secured thru the Corps Area Film Service.

The 32 camps are also erecting their own educational buildings, which are being rushed to completion under direction of Capt. R. E. Kuhlman.

Feed 300 Men in 17 Minutes

Fast as they lined up, the outdoor kitchen crew fed 300 members of the fire fighting training school held at Co. 903, La Canada, Calif. Mess Steward Ludwig's gang fed 300 of them in 17 minutes.

The mess crew was equipped with

Will Need 100,000 Men to Fill Ranks After June 30

The CCC will be expanded to include 299,800 enrollees between July 1 and July 20, in compliance with instructions transmitted by the War Department to corps area headquarters during the past week. Included in this number will be 265,780 juniors, 27,200 war veterans and 6820 project assistants.

Some 25,000 to 30,000 men will be shipped from the eastern states to camps in the west, after preliminary conditioning at three large reception areas to be opened in the First, Second and Third corps areas.

Ninth corps area will have more camps than any other corps area. There will be 211 eastern companies working in the Ninth corps area during the second half of the enrollment period. With 102 local companies, the corps area will contain 313 camps. Fourth corps area will have 236 camps; Eighth,

No Three Month's Service in West

Enrollees who came into the corps in April of this year will not be eligible for assignment to a company being moved outside the corps area of its origin unless the enrollee agrees in writing that he will remain in the CCC until at least Dec. 31, 1938.

Purpose of this is to reduce the possibility of having to pay return expenses to men who might decide to leave the corps after the expiration of his first six months. If he is kept in his home corps area it won't cost the Government so much to effect his discharge and return home.

The form the enrollee will sign will be something like this, addressed to the commanding general of his corps area: "I request that my current enrollment, which has entered into by me on April ——, 1938, and which will expire normally on October ——, 1938, be extended to a period terminating not earlier than Dec. 31, 1938."

209; Seventh, 208; Sixth, 141; Third, 129; Fifth, 116; Second, 81 and the First, 67.

The Fourth corps area will organize the largest number of companies, 284. The Seventh will enroll 229; Fifth, 173; Eighth, 162; Sixth, 162; Third, 153; Second, 146; Ninth, 102 and the First, 89.

From the First corps area in the Eighth, there will be 22 companies; from the Third, 24 and from the Seventh, one. In the Ninth corps area will be: Second corps area companies, 65; Fourth, 48; Fifth, 57; Sixth, 21; Seventh, 20.

It is expected there will be room for 100,000 new men in the corps after July 1. Conditioning camps will be located at Fort Devens in Massachusetts, Camp Dix, New Jersey and at a new camp at Tobyhanna, Pa. Into these camps will go those men destined for shipment to the camps in the Eighth and Ninth corps areas.

Such conditioning camps were used extensively during the early years of the CCC. New enrollees are given preliminary physical training, are outfitted and gain an opportunity of becoming accustomed to camp life before being sent any long distance from their homes.

Department of Agriculture camps during the period (excepting Soil Conservation Corps camps) will number 713. SCS will man 360 camps; Department of the Interior, 421 and the

(Continued on Page 17)

First It Was LEM's; Now It'll Be PA's

Project assistants will be selected beginning July 1. This position, au-

MEMBERS

Arbogast, Howard
Bigler, Jack
Bowers, Ray
Campbell, Lee
Cavalier, Frank
Cost, Dominick
Davis, Harley
Detson, William
Fortney, Paul
Gower, Paul
Harper, Trent
Hennesy, Phillip
Hustead, Ervin
Keruskin, Pete
Kirby, John
Louden, Dennis
McCormick, H.
Montgomery, B.
Moore, Paul W.
Oliveto, Tony
Posey, Hubert
Powell, Junior
Pritt, Lee
Reese, Berten
Roby, Robert
Rozewicz, Louie
Skelley, John
Smith, Arthur
Starkey, Oris
Strother, Wayman
Thornton, Albert
Vance, Roy
Weisend, Robert
Woods, Harry

Ashcraft, R.
Bitonti, Lewis
Bruno, Frank A.
Carroll, John E.
Chiera, Wilmer
Cottrill, C.
Dodge, Robert
Edmond, Randall
Goodwin, Paul
Greaver, William
Heldreth, W. F.
Henry, Carl
Johnson, Roy
Kimes, Herbert
Kovaly, Andy
Manns, Thomas
Meritt, Alaska
Moore, Raymond
Moran, Elbert
Pendry, Walter
Pouch, Stanley
Powers, Elmer
Pyles, Albert
Richards, Edgar
Rodriguez, H.
Shifflett, Ed.
Slider, Harlan
Smith, Edward
Streight, Harry
Sutton, John
Turner, Carl
Wagner, Orvil
Wilfong, Earl

Bartosh, Felix
Bohon, Charles
Burns, Junior
Casto, Robert
Conrad, Woodrow
Cumberledge, C.
Dolog, Andy
Fetty, Robert
Gower, Cledith
Haney, Oscar F.
Henline, Lawson
Hoffman, James
Kavosick, Amiel
Kirby, Ellsworth
Long, Leroy H.
Marquess, Arthur
Miller, Guy
Moore, Lowell
Myers, Edward O.
Petroski, Frank
Powell, Harry
Price, Lewis
Pyles, Richard
Riley, Daniel
Romano, Armando
Simms, Herbert
Sloan, William
Spencer, Don
Strother, Dessil
Tate, Louis
Watson, Gale
Wilt, Woodrow
Young, Jack E.
Yeager, Stewart

THANKSGIVING

CCC Company 3520
Camp S-72
Elkwater, W. Virginia
1936

MENU

Fruit Cocktail
Roast Turkey
Turkey Dressing -- Giblet Gravy
Mashed Potatoes
Celery - Cranberry Sauce - Olives
Head Lettuce Salad
Cinnamon Rolls -Coffee
Mince Meat Pie -- Chocolate Ice Cream
Candy -- Cigars

COURTESY OF THE KELLOGG COMPANY, BATTLE CREEK, MICHIGAN

ARMY PERSONNEL

Commanding Officer

W. H. Unger, 1st Lt. Engr-Res. 38th Engr.

Junior Officer

C. B. Voegtlin, 2nd Lt. FA-Res. 325th FA.

Medical Officer

A. H. Hendricks, -------- Capt. Med-Res.

Educational Adviser

Mr. Carroll A. Bond

TECHNICAL SERVICE

Camp Superintendent ------ Donald L. Lord
Engineer ------------------- Ralph Lawhorn
Mechanic -------------------- Ray Argabrite
Blacksmith ------------------- C. D. Fox
Machine Operator ---------- Bernard Isner
Junior Foreman ------------- W. A. Skaggs
Junior Foreman ----------- Oliver Hamilton
Junior Foreman ----------- Marvin Stalnaker
Junior Foreman ------------- J.R. Tolley
Squad Foreman ----------- Clawson Scott
Squad Foreman ------- --- Virgil Belcher

ARMY OVERHEAD

LEADERS

Frum, James Elmer ------- Senior Foreman.
Goade, Romey --------------- Mess Steward.
Switzer, Henry - ------------ 1st Cook.
Swisher, Arthur --- ---------- 1st Cook.
Tovis, Joseph ------------- Store Keeper.

Ass't Leaders

Simmons, Adrian ------------- Truck Driver
Obertance, Frank --------------- 2nd Cook
Gatain, Wayne ------------------ Co. Clerk
Spence, Denver ------------- First Aid Att.
Ashton, Robert -------------- Ass't Ed. Adv.
Kress, Gilbert ------------------ 2nd Cook
Pritt, Ralph ----------------------- Baker

MEMBERS

Curnutte, Jr.
Menear, Roy
Repass, Bill

Hoskins, T. H.
Pack, Willie
Ross, Charles
Phillips, H. W.

Ireson, Robert
Paletta, John
Sarafini, Romey

TECHNICAL SERVICE OVERHEAD

LEADERS		
Anderson, L.	Powers, Elmer	Hustead, Clair
Kyle, Walter	Pryseski, Chas.	McMillan, John
Chance, Gordon	Sines, Cecil	Powell, Junior
Pingley, B. F.		Robinson, C.
ASS'T LEADERS	**MEMBERS**	Romano, Armando
Kenney, Ira	Bourne, Brooks	Shields, C.
Lucas, William	Burner, Kirk	Stewart, Bruce
Pritt, Clarence	Channell Eddie	Stewart, Virgil
	Dailey, Paul	Vertec, Andy
	Halpenny, Chas.	

LOCAL EXPERIENCED MEN

Brunty, Herbert
Currence, Albert
Anderson, Lonnie

English, Frank
Poling, Perry
Pingley, B. F.
Cutlip, Adam W.

Turner, Stanley
Updike, Harold
Pritt, Clarence

Preparing for a snipe hunt for new members at the Nine Mile Camp, Lolo National Forest, Montana.

Enrollees from Ohio examine hot springs at Yellowstone National Park, Wyoming, 1940. They are from Company 535, NP-1. NA

Enrollees stage an entertainment at a Pennsylvania camp in 1933. Social life consisted mainly of going to town on weekends—if the camp was near a town. USFS

Russell P. Borkus

**Menu
and
Roster**

Company 947, C. C. C.
Camp Moran, SP-1
Olga, Washington

**Christmas
1939**

A menu and roster from Company 947, Camp Moran, SP-1, Olga, Washington, for Christmas Day, 1939. The bill of fare included shrimp cocktail, roast turkey, mashed and sweet potatoes, pineapple cheese salad, peas, rolls, mince and cherry pies, fruit cake, ice cream, coffee, nuts, candies and dinner mints. NACCCA

The CCC camps put on exhibits at many shows and fairs. This one was staged by Camp Custer, Michigan, 1939. NA

Parades were a way of advertising CCC accomplishments and goals. This was a July 4th parade at Coeur d'Alene, Idaho, with participants from Company 546, Camp F-113, Hudlow Creek, Idaho. USFS

Inter-camp competition in Michigan. USFS

An outdoor shower at Company 1789, Pactola, South Dakota, 1933. NA

Doing laundry was a weekly chore. NA

A barber provides a shave at Glady Camp, Monongahela National Forest, West Virginia, 1933. USFS

Cartoons that appeared in Happy Days, drawn by Martin Filchock of Company 1333, Poe Valley, Pennsylvania.

MARTIN FILCHOCK

An original comic strip that appeared during CCC days. Martin Filchock, who served with Company 1333, Poe Valley, Pennsylvania, is a well-known freelance artist today. MARTIN FILCHOCK

Front page copy of the *Camp Cade Courier* of Company 516, Camp NP-4, Mammoth Cave, Kentucky, Oct. 1, 1935. Camp newsletters ranged from crude to sophisticated and thousands were published in the Corps' nine-year history. HUGH WEBER

Enrollee Walter Shadesty, of Wrangell, Alaska, wears a Potlatch button blouse with frog design. He worked in the Tongass National Forest. Most Alaska CCC enrollees were natives who worked during the day and returned to their homes at night. USFS

War veterans at leisure in a state park camp near San Leandro, California, 1933. NA

Company 570, a veterans camp whose enrollees served in California and Idaho, 1934. EASTERN WASHINGTON HISTORICAL SOCIETY

Interior of a tent barracks at
the La Croix Side Camp,
Superior National Forest,
Minnesota, 1940. USFS

A group of black enrollees at
a camp in Northern Idaho,
1933. EASTERN WASHINGTON
HISTORICAL SOCIETY

Enrollees at a camp in the
St. Maries, Idaho district,
1933. EASTERN WASHINGTON
HISTORICAL SOCIETY

World Premiere

"WE'RE ALL IN THE CCC's NOW"

(A Comedy of Life in the CCC)

FEATURING

JOHN SIMMONS, PAUL SIPES

AND

MISS JEANNE GRIFFITH

With 200 CCC Enrollees From Trinity National Forest
And A Fine Supporting Cast From Trinity High
Weaverville, California

High School Gymnasium

Monday Night

MAY 2, 1938

Admission FREE   8 p.m.

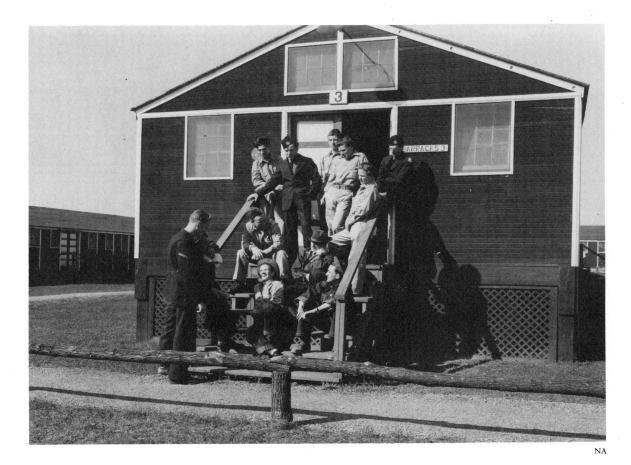

The mascot of Camp F-41, Columbia National Forest, Washington, gets attention befitting a native son of Washington, 1933. USFS

Crews planting trees on cut-over and slash-burned land in the Lolo National Forest, Montana, 1938. This job was one of the primary projects of the CCC in the west. LC

WORK PROJECTS

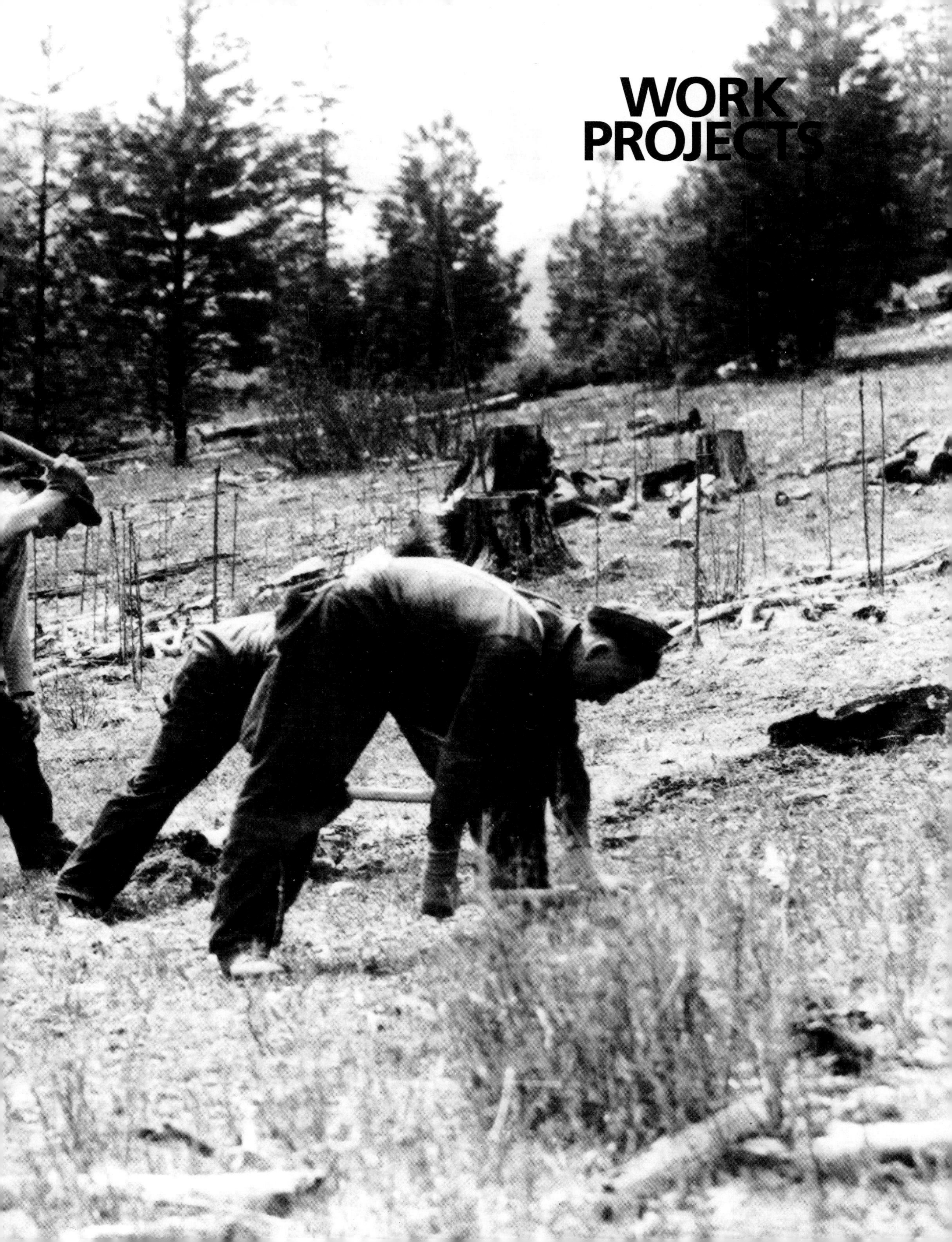

Work projects during the CCC's nine-year history were as varied as the men doing them. Originally, the projects were confined to forestry, park development, and soil erosion control, but later they included disaster relief, historical restoration, and national defense.

The CCC advanced the cause of conservation work by many years; it saved millions of acres of forest and crop land that were in danger of being lost forever. Without this action of the 1930s, later generations would have paid a high price in the loss of vital natural resources.

The following list illustrates some of the work accomplished between 1933 and 1942:

Telephone Lines Laid . . . . 89,000 Miles
Fire Lookout Towers 3,400
Fighting Forest Fires . . . . More than 6 million
                                        man-days
Fire Breaks . . . . 68,000 miles
Public Campground Development . . . 52,000 acres
Range Revegetation . . . . 814,000 acres
Stocking Fish . . . . 972 million
Foot Trails . . . . 13,100 miles
Stream and Lake Bank Protection . . . . 154 million
                                    square yards
Historic Restoration . . . . 3,980 structures
Mosquito Control . . . . 248,000 acres
Timber Estimating . . . . 35 million acres
Trees Planted . . . . More than 2 billion

Henry A. Wallace, who was vice-president of the United States from 1941 to 1945 and served before that as Roosevelt's Secretary of Agriculture, summed up the conservation picture of the country in the early 1930s with these words:

> Thoughtlessly we have destroyed or wounded a considerable part of our common wealth in this country. We have ripped open and to some extent devitalized more than half of all the land in the United States. We have slashed down forests and loosed floods upon ourselves. We have torn up grassland and left the earth to blow away. We have shallowed and befouled our creeks, rivers, and other living waters. We have built great reservoirs and power plants and let them be crippled with silt and debris, long before they have been paid for.

Here is a summary of work projects conducted by the various federal agencies with which the CCC was affiliated:

DEPARTMENT OF AGRICULTURE

The Department of Agriculture was founded in 1862 and was responsible for Federal agricultural policy, soil erosion control, and administration of the national forests. Henry A. Wallace and Claude Wickard were the secretaries of Agriculture during the CCC days.

UNITED STATES FOREST SERVICE

The U.S. Forest Service was established in 1905 and was charged with the administration of national forest reserves throughout the country. Its primary responsibilities in the early days were forest protection and timber management. The overwhelming number of CCC camps were on national forest land and they contributed greatly to the protection and management of the forests. In the 1930s, 150 national forests were located in 39 states, the largest being in the West. There were also national forests in Alaska and Puerto Rico.

The Forest Service was also in charge of CCC camps on state and private forests. In Alaska and Puerto Rico the Forest Service had administrative control of all camps on national forest lands, while the War Department controlled most other camps).

The Forest Service provided some of the project supervisors and determined what projects should be undertaken. The first CCC camp was in the George Washington National Forest, Virginia, and all camps in national forests had "F" as part of their camp designation.

In addition to fighting fires and planting trees, CCC boys in thinned dense timber stands and worked on expanding seed production, forest recreation projects, blister rust control, insect and disease damage, road building, and many other projects related to forest management.

FIRE FIGHTING

The first priority of the CCC was the protection of the country's vast forest resources. Organized fire fighting was developed in the national forest system with the formation of the U.S. Forest Service in 1905, but lack of funds and manpower through the years limited what the Forest Service could do.

The CCC's fight against fires was two-fold. With the vast manpower available from the Corps, trained people could man the fire lines along with regular Forest Service personnel. The other aspect of fire fighting was fire prevention. CCC enrollees built fire breaks, roads, fire lookouts, and airfields, installed telephone lines, cleared debris and patrolled forest areas. All of this contributed tremendously to the war against fires as did the CCC's work on insect and disease control and slash disposal.

Building a fire tower on Strawberry Mountain, Fremont National Forest, Oregon, 1933. USFS

All enrollees involved in fire fighting were trained before being allowed on the fire lines. Each company had its own picked squad and its area to protect. Range and grass fires were also fought by CCC men stationed in soil erosion camps. National Park Service camps were responsible for protection in the parks.

Fire fighting was not done without cost. Twenty-nine enrollees were killed fighting fires in nine years. Of these, 10 were lost fighting the Blackwater fire on the Shoshone National Forest in Wyoming in August 1937.

SOIL CONSERVATION SERVICE

The Soil Erosion Service, established in 1933, was originally under the Interior Department, but in 1935 was transferred to the Agriculture Department and its name changed to Soil Conservation Service. Its main purpose was to help farmers and ranchers use land and water resources to reduce flood and erosion loss. It was responsible for flood prevention, drainage and irrigation, and watershed protection on millions of acres, especially in the country's mid-section.

During the early 1930s, a great natural disaster was occurring in the rich farm land extending from the Rocky Mountains east to the flatlands of Illinois, and from Texas north to Iowa and Nebraska. This was the famous "Dust Bowl" era. Drastic steps were required.

Hundreds of camps were established in the affected areas, with most of the enrollees coming from nearby farming communities. Gully control, tree planting, levee repairs, tile drains, and other projects helped control erosion on millions of acres of farmland that otherwise would have been abandoned to the ravages of nature.

By June 1936, the SCS had 147 demonstration projects averaging 25 to 30,000 acres, 48 soil conservation nurseries, 23 research stations and 454 CCC camps working on soil erosion projects.

Other agencies of the Department of Agriculture that were involved with CCC work were the Bureau of Agricultural Engineering, which assisted public drainage organizations with maintenance and improvements and the Bureau of Biological Survey which worked on wildlife restoration.

TENNESSEE VALLEY AUTHORITY

The Tennessee Valley Authority was created in 1933 to develop the resources of the Tennessee River Valley in Tennessee, Kentucky, Alabama, Virginia, Mississippi, and North Carolina. Dams were built for flood control and electrical power.

CCC enrollees from about 30 camps in the area worked primarily on tree planting and fire fighting.

DEPARTMENT OF THE INTERIOR

The department was established in 1849 and was charged with the custody of the nation's natural resources. Harold L. Ickes was the secretary throughout the Roosevelt administrations.

NATIONAL PARK SERVICE

The National Park Service was established in 1916 under the Department of the Interior. The first national

Flood control work in Utah. UTAH STATE HISTORICAL SOCIETY

CCC enrollees building a
dam near Las Cruces,
Colorado. COLORADO
HISTORICAL SOCIETY

Enrollees building fences in
Colorado. COLORADO
HISTORICAL SOCIETY

An enrollee cultivates young
trees at a nursery for
shelterbelt plantings on the
Lower Souris National
Wildlife Refuge, North
Dakota, 1941. NA

park in the country was Yellowstone, established in 1872. Since then, many natural, archeological and historical areas have been set aside as parks. Conrad Wirth was the Park Service director during the 1930s and 1940s.

Next to the U.S. Forest Service, the National Park Service was perhaps the greatest participant in CCC projects. It has been said that without CCC help, it would have taken 50 years to accomplish what was done in nine years.

Nearly 50 national parks and monuments used CCC labor. These ranged from one end of the country to the other and included Hot Springs, Arkansas; Grand Canyon, Arizona; Mt. McKinley, Alaska; Lassen Volcanic, Sequoia, and Yosemite, California; Mesa Verde and Rocky Mountain, Colorado; Bryce Canyon and Zion, Utah; Crater Lake, Oregon; Ft. McHenry, Maryland; Hawaii Volcanoes, Hawaii; Mt. Rainier, Washington; Platt, Oklahoma; Wind Cave, South Dakota; Yellowstone and Grand Teton, Wyoming; Great Smoky, North Carolina and Tennessee; Shenandoah, Virginia; Acadia, Maine; and Carlsbad Caverns, New Mexico. Mammoth Cave in Kentucky was established in 1941 after the CCC had built roads and erosion, dams, and improved the Cave's interior. Before this, a private company had led tours through the cave. This was one park for which the CCC was directly responsible.

The CCC provided manpower and materials to build thousands of shelters, picnic areas, swimming pools, and other recreational facilities, water and sewage systems, administrative structures, museums, historic restorations, roads, as well as manpower for reforestation and soil erosion control work.

In 1935, more than 500 camps were operating on Park Service projects. By 1936 more than 300 camps were operating at state and local parks.

State and Local Parks
State park development was in its infancy in the early 1900s. By 1921 only 19 states had state park systems, but with the coming of automobile travel, state officials faced a real demand for parks and campgrounds. By the middle 1920s all 48 states had started some kind of development. By 1930, however, the depression had all but stopped the activity. With establishment of the CCC, development of state, municipal and rural parks was resumed. Many state park systems really got their second start from CCC activity.

This was also the period when "rustic" architecture became the dominant style in park construction. Logs, rustic woodwork, and stone were the major materials used. Natural settings were emphasized.

One of the best examples of CCC architecture is the Big Springs complex, near Van Buren, Missouri, in the Ozark National Scenic Riverways. Twenty-six buildings remain in their original settings around Big Springs, one of the largest natural springs in the country. All of the buildings are built of logs and stone and are maintained by the National Park Service.

A good example of the CCC involvement in state park development was in Virginia. In 1933, the state had only two state parks. By June 1942, the state had developed, with CCC help, 11 additional park areas, and had built roads, water and sewer systems, telephone and power lines, and many recreational structures.

Many other rural and urban parks throughout the country were directly affected by CCC projects. Most of the camps were guided by National Park Service personnel.

Some examples of park development by the CCC are the Combination building at Myrtle Beach State Park, South Carolina; the Administration building at Mohawk Trail State Forest Park, Massachusetts; the Concession building at Longhorn Cavern State Park, Texas; the Boathouse, at Mohawk Metropolitan Park, Tulsa, Oklahoma; the Buildings at the Denver Metropolitan Park, Colorado; the Concession building at Levi Carter State Park, Nebraska; the Lodge at Stone State Park, Iowa; and the Lodge at Davis Mountain State Park, Texas. Projects were completed at Oberlin Sappa State Park in Kansas; Kettlefoot and Booker T. Washington State Park in Tennessee; Magnolia Spring State Park in Georgia; and Griffith Park in the Los Angeles area.

Many ski areas were developed or improved, among them Mount Greylock, Massachusetts; Grayling Winter Sports Park, Michigan; Rite Mountain, Wisconsin; Casper Mountain, Wyoming; and Hyde State Park, New Mexico.

General Land Office
The General Land Office operated six camps in the West and Alaska. One of the most unusual of the CCC projects in the country was the camp set up in the coal fields of Little Thunder Basin, Wyoming, near Gillette, to fight the fires that had burned in the immense coal fields there for hundreds of years.

Several reforestation camps were set up in Oregon. In 1940, the General Land Office took over millions of acres in Alaska and established projects there for Alaskan Indians and Eskimos. They helped more than 100 native villages with sewer and water services, clean-up and road and trail construction. There was no age or marital restrictions. Enrollees lived in their own villages.

Office of Indian Affairs
The Office of Indian Affairs participated in the CCC program, and more than 88,000 men of Indian ancestry

Starting work on the foundation for a community kitchen in the Columbia National Forest, Washington, 1936. USFS

French Creek Camp F-1090. Enrollees chopping insect-killed timber into firewood, Idaho National Forest, Idaho, 1938. USFS

served. All the work was performed on Indian reservations and the enrollees lived at their homes. CCC regulations were changed considerably to meet the realities of reservation life. The War Department was not involved with camp administration.

Work was performed on nearly 300 tracts of land in 23 states. The purpose was to provide employment for Indians who had never had steady jobs and to bring conservation to the Indian reservations. Thousands of Indians learned job skills. Important conservation work was accomplished.

BUREAU OF RECLAMATION

The Bureau of Reclamation was responsible for water resources in the West. It designed and built engineering works to provide irrigation and electrical power.

Under the Reclamation Act of 1902, many dams and irrigation channels had been built, but by 1933 these systems were in a state of disrepair.

The CCC set up camps to rehabilitate these systems and to build dams, clear reservoir sites, excavate canals and build other water control structures. Enrollees worked on disaster relief after floods, prairie grass fires and insect infestations. They also improved recreational areas.

There were camps in 15 western states. The enrollees cleared 39,000 acres of reservoir sites, built 15,800 water control structures on canals and ditches, and repaired and cleaned millions of square yards of canals and drainage ditches. This work greatly contributed to the agriculture economy of the areas, providing better growing conditions.

GRAZING SERVICE

Dozens of camps were established on 58 grazing districts in 10 western states. Work was performed in accordance with the objectives of the Taylor Grazing Act, which was passed to improve the grazing lands of the West.

Major projects were water hole construction, reseeding of burned over range land, road building to facilitate the movement of cattle, fence building to control grazing land, surveying and map making, fire suppression and the control of insects and predatory animals.

FISH AND WILDLIFE SERVICE

The two main functions of CCC projects with the Fish and Wildlife Service were the improvement of wildlife habitat and construction of administrative facilities. Like other aspects of conservation in the United States, wildlife areas and refuges were in need of repair and improvement.

Forty-four of the more than 200 wildlife refuges in the country were built by the CCC. Enrollees constructed dams, dikes and other water control impoundments, planted cover vegetation and millions of trees for windbreaks, stabilized stream banks, erected many buildings, fire lookout towers, and fences, installed telephone lines, and built fire breaks.

The CCC contributed greatly to the protection and advancement of the wildlife and fish resources of the country.

CCC boys re-enact an attempted breakthrough of Confederate lines at the Petersburg National Battlefield Park in Virginia in 1940. This was done for well-known author, Douglas Southall Freeman, who wrote *Lee's Lieutenants, A Study in Command.* AC

Rookies in training for firefighting at Camp Roosevelt, Virginia, 1940. USFS

Road work on the Bitterroot National Forest, Montana, 1933. USFS

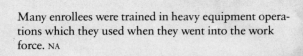

Many enrollees were trained in heavy equipment operations which they used when they went into the work force. NA

WAR DEPARTMENT

The War Department was in charge of all camp administration and transportation to the camps, excluding the ones in the territories. Its nine-year involvement with the CCC provided a vast pool of trained regular and reserve Army officers in World War II. The three million enrollees provided the military services with hundreds of job skills.

The Army Corps of Engineers used the CCC on two huge projects. The Winooski River in Vermont and the Walkill River in New York had caused millions of dollars of flood damage. Three dams were constructed on the Winooski River in the 1930s using CCC labor, supervised by the Corps of Engineers. This greatly reduced the flood menace in the area. In 1937, the Walkill River channelling and levee construction were completed. This work prevented the flood waters from inundating rich crop lands of the Walkill River Valley.

By 1940, CCC projects generally had a national defense orientation, and by the CCC's demise in June 1942, most of the remaining camps were on military bases.

DISASTER RELIEF

The CCC was used extensively in disaster relief.

The great Ohio-Mississippi rivers flood of 1937 was a real test. Enrollees built sandbag dikes up and down the rivers and helped rescue and evacuate thousands of flood victims. Cleanup was conducted after flood water receded. Many other major floods of the 1930s were likewise attacked and controlled by CCC enrollees.

The great New England hurricane of 1938 killed more than 500 people and caused more than $400 million damage. The CCC helped in the cleanup and repair of more than 14,000 houses and buildings.

In the greatest hurricane ever to strike the Florida Keys, on September 2, 1935, the CCC helped in the clean up, retrieved bodies of victims, and suffered its own greatest disaster. Veterans Camp No. 5 on Lower Matecumbe Key was demolished and more than 200 of the 716 veteran enrollees were killed. Their camp was not built to withstand the tremendous winds of the hurricanes prevalent in the area.

In many other disasters, from tornados and floods to snowstorms and plane crashes, the CCC helped in cleanup, rescue work, building repair, and the depressing job of retrieving bodies. Enrollees were used in the search for a kidnapped child in Florida in 1938. The search ended tragically when the child was found dead.

HISTORICAL RESTORATION

The cultural heritage of the country was not neglected

Surveying was one of the subjects taught to enrollees who wanted a career after their stint in the CCC. USFS

by the CCC. Fort Necessity near Pittsburgh, Pennsylvania, built in 1754 by George Washington and surrendered to the French during the French and Indian War, was reconstructed. One of the outstanding physical restorations by the CCC was the complete rebuilding of La Purisimia Mission in California, originally erected by the Spanish in 1787. Prior to construction of Boulder (now Hoover) Dam on the Colorado River, the CCC participated in extensive archeological excavations around the dam site. It also worked on another important archeological site at Mound State Park near Moundville, Alabama. The National Park Service and the CCC did extensive rehabilitation work at Gettysburg National Military Park in Pennsylvania and Yorktown National Military Park in Virginia. The CCC had the distinction of firing the last shot of the Civil War, when it found and deliberately detonated a live cannon shell at Gettysburg.

The CCC built museums such as those at Ft. Churchill State Park in Nevada, Ginko Petrified State Park in Washington, Custer State Park in South Dakota, a branch of the Wyoming State Museum at Guernsey, and Hawks Nest State Park in West Virginia. They helped clean and clear the historic C and O Canal historical area in Maryland, West Virginia and the District of Columbia.

One of the most unusual and interesting of the historical projects was in Alaska. Many of the ancient totem poles of southeastern Alaska were in a bad state of repair. Beginning in 1938, 48 old poles were restored, 54 were duplicated, and 19 new ones were carved and set up at the Sitka National Monument. Archeological exploration was also conducted on the site of the Russian settlement at old Sitka, site of an Indian-inspired massacre in 1802.

ROAD AND TRAIL CONSTRUCTION

Road and trail construction was a very important part of CCC work in the forests, parks and rangelands. The CCC also worked under National Park Service direction on parkway development around metropolitan and historical areas. It helped build the Illinois Parkway, following the old Illinois-Michigan Canal from Chicago to LaSalle, Illinois; the Veterans Memorial Parkway between Bay City and Saginaw, Michigan; the Rahway River Parkway in New Jersey; and parkways around Cleveland, Ohio and Milwaukee, Wisconsin.

The Appalachian Trail from Maine to Georgia and the Pacific Crest Trail in California were improved and expanded by CCC labor.

TERRITORIAL PROJECTS

The United States territories of Alaska, Hawaii, Puerto Rico, and the Virgin Islands each had CCC projects and some permanent camps. In Alaska, unemployment affected the middle-aged man rather than the youth, so no age or re-enrollment restrictions were imposed. However, a one-year residence was required for enrollment. Camps were small because of the distances involved. Indian and Eskimo enrollees lived at their homes and worked on projects during the day. Projects were scattered from one end of Alaska to the other. They included roads and trails for recreation, stream gauging stations, bridges, historical restorations, burning on the right-of-way of the Alaska Railroad and fire fighting. Many useful projects were conducted in interior Alaska. Drainage ditches, wells, landing fields, herder's shelter cabins, cold storage facilities, and telephone lines were built. The CCC built a muskox corral on Nuniwak Island and razed an old Army barracks at St. Michael, as well as flood drainage cleanup and soil erosion work.

In 1940, the CCC, along with Army engineers, built the Annette Island Air Field in southeastern Alaska, a major contribution to Alaskan defense.

In Hawaii, territory residents were employed in tree planting, fire break construction and improvement of recreation areas.

Puerto Rico and the Virgin Islands had some camps. The work was mainly reforestation, road building, and construction of recreational facilities.

In its nine-year history, the CCC had approximately 50,000 enrollees from the territories.

Crew from Camp Angeles Crest, F-133, California, who worked on an erosion control project on the Angeles Crest Highway, 1934. USFS

Crew from Camp NP-4 at Babb, Montana, repairs siphon tubes that transferred water from the St. Mary's River (Hudson Bay drainage) to the Milk River (Gulf of Alaska drainage), 1934. MONTANA HISTORICAL SOCIETY

Members of the Whitehall Drouth Relief Camp, Montana, rebuild a fence, 1934. USFS

Reconditioning a trail near Hoonah, Alaska, on the Tongass National Forest. USFS

Snags were felled to reduce the fire hazard in the Columbia National Forest, Washington. USFS

Thousands of miles of forest trails were built or cleaned up in the national forests of the United States. This is a trail in the Wasatch National Forest, Utah.
UTAH STATE HISTORICAL SOCIETY

Archaeological work on old Sitka, Alaska, in the Tongass National Forest, 1935. USFS

CCC men sandbag the Mississippi at Cates Landing near Tystonville, Tennessee, during the great Ohio-Mississippi River flood of 1937. NA

Erosion control on Trout Creek Pass, Cochetopa National Forest, Colorado, 1933. Cloudbursts wreaked havoc on slopes in this area. USFS

Men from Camp SCS-7, Warrenton, Oregon, erect a picket fence along the seashore for sand dune control, 1941. NA

Flood control work was a major project of the CCC. There was a working agreement between the CCC and the American Red Cross for disaster relief throughout the United States in the early 1940s. AMERICAN RED CROSS

Hundreds of fire lookouts were built by the CCC in the national and state forests and parks throughout the country. Fire prevention and fire fighting were two of the main responsibilities of the CCC in the nation's parks and forests. NA

A typical log structure built by the CCC in Lassen National Park, California, 1934. NPS

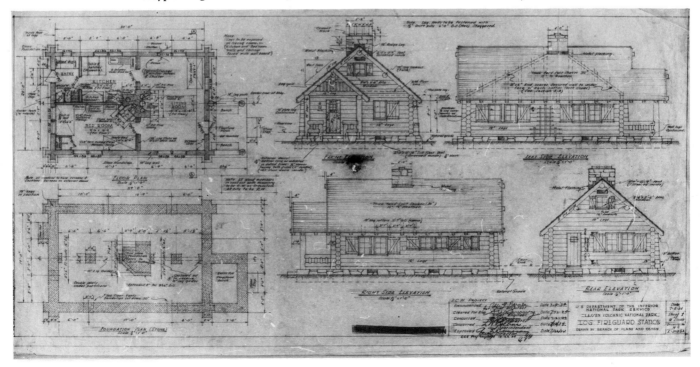

A new office and warehouse at Silver Lake Ranger Station, Fremont National Forest, Oregon. USFS

A new warehouse in the Nicolet National Forest, Wisconsin. USFS

A shelter built in Pierre, South Dakota, 1936 — one of thousands built in the national parks and forests from 1933 to 1942 by the CCC. USFS

A crew rehabilitates a house in the Sumter National Forest, South Carolina, 1938. USFS

Constructing a guard station, Boise National Forest, Idaho. USFS

A log cabin being built as a recreational center for the CCC and the Animal Husbandry Farm in Maryland, 1934. USFS

Forester's office at the China Flat CCC Camp, Oregon, 1936. USFS

Fitting logs for the La Croix Guard Station in the Superior National Forest, Minnesota, 1940. USFS

Building Ashburnham Camp F-13, Massachusetts, 1939. Enrollees built their own camps all over the country. USFS

Sewer lines and a water supply ditch built by the CCC on Annette Island, Alaska, 1940. NA

Planting trees around Little Round Top, Gettysburg National Military Park, Pennsylvania, 1936. NA

Enrollees reproduce colonial furniture at Yorktown National Historical Park, Virginia. NA

Manufacturing portable
stoves at the Gasquet CCC
camp, Siskiyou National
Forest, Oregon, 1941. USFS

Men from Camp FWS-2
construct a utility building
on the Bosque del Apache
Migratory Waterfowl
Refuge, Arizona, 1940. NA

Enrollees from Camp
F-53N, Glorieta, New
Mexico, helped stabilize
these ruins at Pecos Mission,
1940. NA

Enrollees operate jackhammers at a quarry on Annette Island, Alaska, Tongass National Forest, 1941. USFS

Grading the Mameyes, Rio Blanco Road, Caribbean National Forest, Puerto Rico. USFS

Construction on the Danby Road near Danby, Vermont, in the Green Mountain National Forest, 1933. USFS

Digging out limestone for surfacing truck trails in Dean State Forest near Lawrenceville, Ohio, 1934.

A class in beekeeping at Camp CP-2, Peekskill, New York. NA

Building fly traps to put in camp bathrooms at Cowan's Gap Camp in Pennsylvania, 1933. USFS

Enrollees from Company 535, Camp NP-1, lay cement in a utility building at Mammoth Springs, Yellowstone National Park, Wyoming, 1940. NA

Building a new entrance to New Market Campground, George Washington National Forest, Virginia, 1933. USFS

Men from Camp SCS-10, Weiser, Idaho, work on installation of a telephone line from their camp to Weiser, 1941. NA

Rock wall construction on the south rim of Grand Canyon National Park, Arizona. NPS

Stream improvement near the Campton Pond Forest Camp, White Mountain National Forest, New Hampshire, 1938. USFS

Swimming pool construction at the La Mina recreational unit of the Caribbean National Forest, Puerto Rico, 1935. USFS

An enrollee bulldozes a switchback on the north side of Potts Mountain, Jefferson National Forest, Virginia. USFS

TRAINING AND
EDUCATION

The original concept of the Civilian Conservation Corps was to put unemployed youths to work on natural resource projects. The Corps was an emergency work force managed by the Army; little thought was given to education or training other than what was needed to get the job done. Eventually, though, the CCC evolved into an agency that not only gave mass employment opportunities to youth but also provided both vocational training and academic instruction.

Many of the young men employed by the CCC had dropped out of school, often because they could not afford to continue. A large percentage, especially the black recruits from the South, could not read or write, or were deficient in these basic skills. This was a real disadvantage, especially for youths who were required to operate machines or perform technical jobs. The average schooling for recruits in 1935 was 8.7 years. Many recruits had no vocational training or previous employment experience. Estimates of the number of youths under the age of 25 who were unemployed and out of school vary from three to six million.

The executive order creating the CCC in 1933 did not mention education or training as a function of the new agency. But by the end of 1933, it was apparent that training was essential.

In February 1934, an educational adviser was authorized for each camp, and camp officers, work supervisors, and local schoolteachers were enlisted on a voluntary basis to offer courses to enrollees, usually after working hours. Instruction in vocational and academic subjects was given from elementary through college levels.

When Congress established the CCC as a separate agency in 1937, it included as one of its functions the education of its recruits, and provided for up to 10 hours a week that could be used for general education and vocational training.

Correspondence extension courses were offered to enrollees throughout the agency. A school organized by the educational adviser in California offered 10 extension courses: auto mechanics, business English, diesel engines, elementary aeronautics, forestry, blueprint reading, techniques of study, journalism, practical photography, and psychology. Each course consisted of 12 lessons and the enrollee received a certificate upon completion of the course.

In April 1939, President Roosevelt said of his plan for the reorganization of the government and the CCC: "Its major purpose is to promote the welfare and further the training of the individuals who make up the Corps, important as may be the construction work which they have carried on so successfully."

Through the War Department the federal government controlled all educational activities in the CCC. The U.S. Office of Education acted in an advisory capacity, preparing programs and nominating the educational adviser for each camp.

In the CCC's later years, federal control of the educational program became controversial. All other educational systems in the country were under state or local control, and there was concern that the federal control in the CCC would create a dual educational system. Education nevertheless continued to be under federal control until the end of the CCC in 1942.

The National Defense Act of 1940 changed some of the educational policies of the CCC. National defense training programs in vocational subjects were taught through local school systems. In 1941, enrollees were allowed to take five hours a week of vocational instruction offered by public schools, and thousands of others were taking training courses taught by CCC personnel. Subjects such as radio operating, welding, aircraft maintenance, auto mechanics, and clerking-typing prepared the enrollee for work in defense industries and the military service. When the United States entered World War II, former CCC men provided a great pool of trained manpower for the armed services.

Vocational education was probably the most important part of the enrollee's training. As the CCC grew and took on more complex projects, the range of its job training increased. Building of park structures, bridges, lookout towers, dams, roads, and trails, and fighting forest fires gave the enrollee job training in plumbing, carpentry, electrical wiring, concrete finishing, handling special tools and machines, surveying, landscaping, and many other skilled occupations. Road building trained men in the use of bulldozers and other heavy equipment. Forestry jobs provided training in biological sciences and the use of maps, compass and tools. Thousands of cooks and bakers were trained, proving especially important to the military during World War II. Office skills were gained through placing enrollees in charge of canteens and clerking jobs. Hundreds of different jobs were learned which proved to be the start of many careers after the CCC experience.

Service in the CCC gave the enrollee a much better chance to obtain a job, even though no outside employment agency really coordinated the job-seeking effort.

One advantage of the entire CCC organization lost in teaching enrollees new skills was the fact that once an enrollee learned a skill, he had little chance for job rotation to learn more skills within his work projects. There was no real policy of matching a person's prior skills and interests to a job within the camp's work proj-

CIVILIAN CONSERVATION CORPS

U.C. 530758

Unit Certificate

THIS CERTIFIES THAT _Russell Barkus_ of Company _747_ has satisfactorily completed _12_ hours of instruction in _Foreman Training_ and is therefore granted this Certificate.

Lester H. Anderson
Project Superintendent.

[signature]
Company Commander.

Fred Flanagan
Camp Educational Adviser.

Date _July 1, 1939_   Place _Camp Moran_

6—9671

Civilian Conservation Corps

CORRESPONDENCE EXTENSION SERVICE
FORT LEWIS DISTRICT

This certifies that ___Russell Barkus___

has satisfactorily completed the Correspondence Extension Course in
Vocational Self-Guidance

and is therefore granted this certificate with all the rights and privileges thereto appertaining.

(Date) **November 14, 1938**   _William A. Kimple_
District Educational Adviser

These certificates are typical of those issued to enrollees upon completion of courses taken at camp or by correspondence. NACCCA

ects. It was only by chance that an enrollee was noticed by the company advisors or technical staff and a lot of the enrollee's extra curricular activities were on his own initiative.

Educational and vocational training varied from camp to camp and from year to year. A lot depended on the attitude of the camp commander and his staff, the technical staff, the educational adviser, and the enrollee himself. In general, an enrollee got out of the CCC as much or as little as he wanted. Some joined just for a job or for something to do. Most joined to help themselves and their families. In the process, and largely incidentally, they helped their country.

CORRESPONDENCE EXTENSION SERVICE

Certificate of Completion

IDAHO STATE DEPARTMENT OF EDUCATION
CIVILIAN CONSERVATION CORPS
WORK PROJECTS ADMINISTRATION

This is to certify that _____ CAMILLO BALSAMO _____

a member of Co. _1249_ of the Civilian Conservation Corps, has successfully completed a course of study in

_____ INTERIOR DECORATING _____

and in recognition of this accomplishment is awarded this Certificate.

No. 7992

J.W. Condie
STATE SUPERINTENDENT

Countersigned

Wallace M. Davis
DISTRICT EDUCATIONAL ADVISER CCC, BOISE DISTRICT

COMMANDING OFFICER

A.H. Baird
EDUCATIONAL PROJECTS
WORK PROJECTS ADMINISTRATION

COMPANY COMMANDER

Dated _____ Jan 10, 1940.

A model telephone line built by enrollees at Camp Entiat, F-78, Wenatchee National Forest, Washington, 1941.
USFS

First aid class at Company 765 at Mohall, North Dakota, 1938. NA

Dr. Louis C. Haynes, camp physician at Camp Roosevelt, Virginia, demonstrates to enrollees the use of an improvised tourniquet in a First Aid class. AMERICAN RED CROSS

Trucks lined up for inspection at the Cut Foot Sioux Camp in the Chippewa National Forest, Minnesota, 1940. USFS

A geography class at Company 4465, Newberry, South Carolina, 1938. Thousands of southern blacks found their education opportunities enhanced in the CCC. NA

Each new group of enrollees went through an orientation period of one week to 10 days during which time they were given an opportunity to adjust themselves to their new life. As part of this program each enrollee met the camp educational advisor who recorded their past experiences, ambitions, schooling, results of aptitude tests, etc., and helped them to make the most of the opportunities available. Gegoka Camp, Superior National Forest, Minnesota, 1940. USFS

Model plane makers in a crafts class of Company 1276, SP-61, Hackettstown, New Jersey. NA

Airplane mechanics course in National Defense Training at Camp Sun Valley, Sunbury, Pennsylvania, 1941. NA

An enrollee operates a jig and pattern machine in the camp workshop where he is cutting out a pattern in sheet steel of a saw blade which will act as a guide for sharpening saws used in the shop. Various patterns are cut for other purposes and as he advances in the work, he learns to lay out the pattern on the steel from drawings. NP-1, Company 535, Yellowstone National Park, Wyoming, 1940. NA

An enrollee operating a band saw in the woodworking shop in the educational building at the Gegoka Camp, Superior National Forest, Minnesota, 1940. USFS

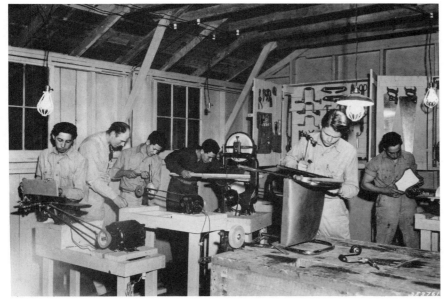

CCC instruction in woodworking and cabinet shop work at Camp F-75, Pine, Arizona, 1939. NA

Enrollees receive instruction in the use of Forest Service radio sets under the direction of the U.S. Office of Education, National Defense Training, in Montana, 1940. USFS

A national defense radio school teaching the Morse Code system at the Huntsville Camp, Cache National Forest, Utah, 1941. USFS

By 1940 a good part of CCC activities were incorporated into the National Defense Training Program. Here is an instructor at Camp Lake Fork, Company 2939, McCall, Idaho, showing a member of a radio repair class how to test a radio set. This defense training was a great help to the wartime call-up of men during World War II. NA

A student enrollee at the Missoula, Montana, national defense auto mechanics training school being instructed by a machinist how to ream out a connecting rod of an automobile motor, 1941. USFS

Radio school, Huntsville Camp, Cache National Forest, Utah, 1941. USFS

Many enrollees learned to type in evening classes in camps throughout the country. This experience would come in handy in both their military and civilian lives. USFS

Taking the oath of enlistment at Wilkes-Barre, Pennsylvania, 1940. NA

LAST YEARS

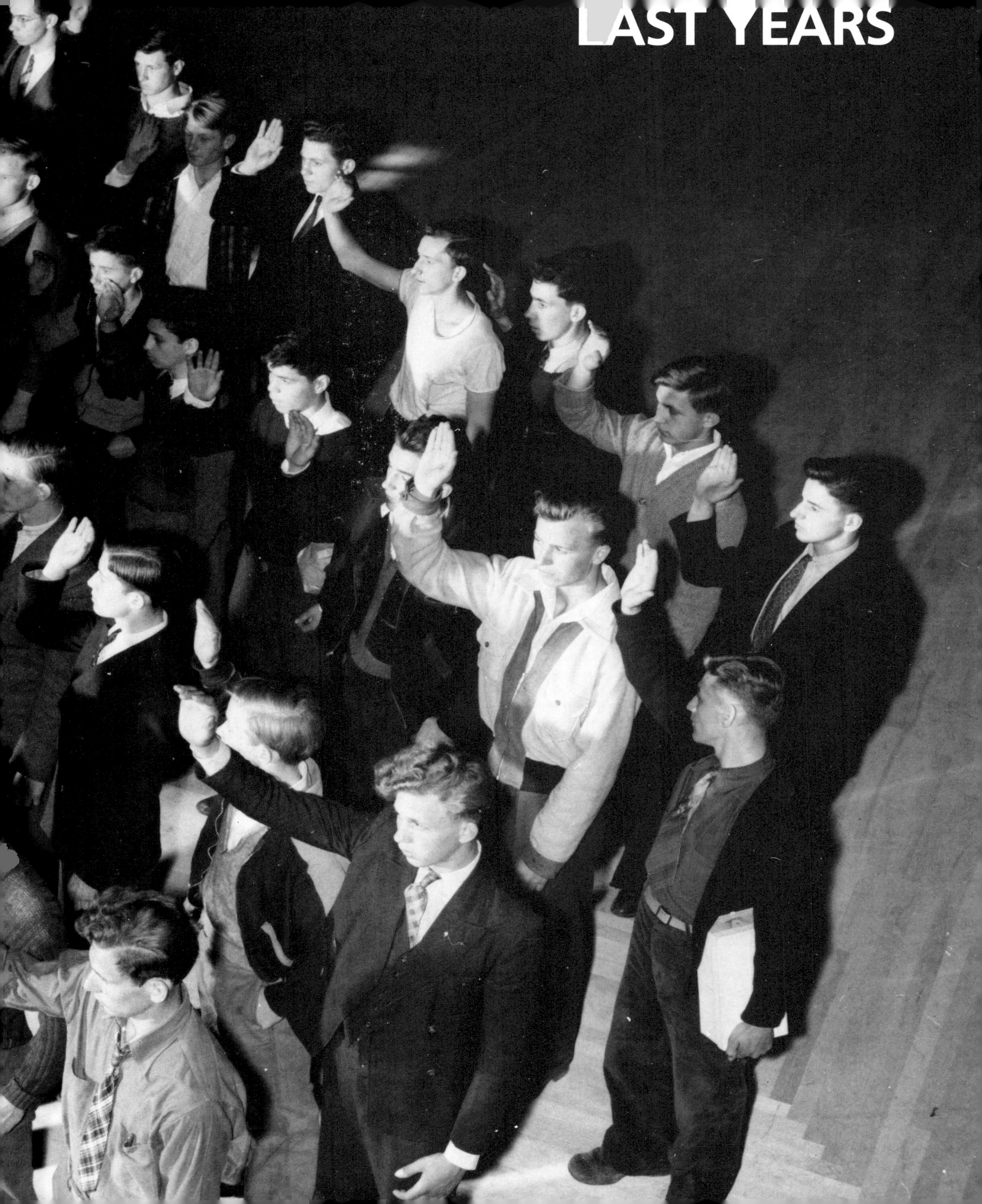

After Robert Fechner's death on January 1, 1940, James D. McEntee assumed the directorship. Although he had been Fechner's assistant since 1933 and knew the organization well, he was not the forceful leader Fechner had been. The CCC concept developed many problems. Not all of them could be laid to McEntee, of course. Times and politics were changing.

The Corps had been basically a relief agency for 6½ years and although there was still unemployment, it was not as severe as it had been. The world political situation had changed. Hitler had taken over part of Central Europe without firing a shot and in September 1939 was ready to crush Poland. Japan, with victories in Asia, was looking to the vast natural resources of Indo-China, the Dutch East Indies, and the Philippines. In the United States, defense spending increased, although the national policy was still isolationist. After Hitler invaded Poland and overran Western Europe, however, the U.S. economy surged upward on the strength of military spending, and unemployment declined dramatically.

In 1939, Congress passed an act assuring continuance of the CCC through June 30, 1943, but not as an independent agency. Instead, it became part of the Federal Security Agency. Under Roosevelt's sweeping reorganization plan, the executive branch of government was divided into three administrative groups: The Federal Security Agency, the Federal Works Agency, and the Federal Loans Agency. Fechner, thinking the CCC should have been placed under the Works Agency, if it couldn't be independent, protested vigorously and even submitted his resignation as director. Roosevelt wouldn't accept it, however, and Fechner stayed on until his death.

Selection of enrollees was transferred from the Labor Department to the Office of the CCC Director. Uniforms were changed from the vintage olive drab left over from World War I to better-tailored outfits of spruce green. This was a definite boost to the enrollees' morale. The War Department's role in administration was somewhat reduced, to the pleasure of the CCC, and reserve Army officers were relieved from active duty with the Corps. Most of them, however, simply switched over to civilian status and stayed on the job.

The CCC was not without its problems in its later years. Segregation was the official policy, especially under Fechner's direction, and the establishment of camps for Negroes produced strong opposition in some areas of the country. Black leaders complained that too few blacks were being enrolled, and that the facilities and training at the Negro camps were inferior.

Influential leaders urged integration, but this never became CCC policy.

Junction of Highways 3 and 10 near Missoula, Montana.

James McEntee, the second director of the CCC, with the Duke of Windsor at Washington, D.C., in September 1941. NA

Several camp mutinies occurred in the East, the result in part of inadequate living conditions, ineffective leadership, and conflict that developed when enrollees from different cultural and economic back grounds were thrown together. Enrollees got into trouble in and out of camp, and there was some criminal activity by camp employees.

In later years, the desertion rate steadily increased. This cost the government millions of dollars, for money was appropriated for each enrollee whether he stayed six months or not. Contributing to this problem were ineffective leadership, lowering of the entrance age to 17—a move that brought in more immature boys— and improving prospects for employment away from the Corps.

Some of these problems were typical of any organization of this size, and did more harm to the CCC's image than to actual operations.

Roosevelt proclaimed a limited national emergency in 1940 after Hitler's troops overran France, and as a result the CCC became more involved in national defense work. Camps were established at many military bases, and more defense-related subjects, such as radio training and aircraft maintenance, were offered in the training program. Military drill was installed, and each enrollee was required to take first-aid training. On the bases, enrollees were put to work building airfields, artillery ranges, ammunition storage buildings and many other military structures. The CCC was no longer just a conservation work force; it had become part of the national defense.

This did not mean, however, that the CCC was be-ing taken over by the military. It never lost sight of its original goal of providing work in conservation projects.

In January 1941, enrollment stood at 300,000, but by the end of the year it had dropped to 160,000, located in 900 camps. As jobs became more plentiful it became harder to recruit enrollees, and pressure increased to combine the CCC with other organizations or to abandon it entirely. Roosevelt, however, wanted to keep the Corps intact at least into 1942.

After December 7, 1941, the CCC offered all its camps to the army for work on military projects, and offered the American Red Cross help with war emergencies. Except for forest fire fighting, all conservation work off military reservations was canceled on January 1, 1942. Two hundred camps were on military reservations and 150 were assigned to fire fighting duty in the West. The manpower drain was tremendous as thousands of enrollees and camp administrators left the CCC to enter military service. Congress faced great pressure to abolish the CCC in 1942. Roosevelt had included in his budget a $49 million appropriation to continue 150 camps, but the House voted 158 to 151 not to appropriate any funds after June 30, 1942. The Senate concurrently voted to retain the Corps, but after further debate, it rescinded this vote and the Corps no longer was funded. After June 30, 1942, it officially went out of existence. The only appropriation left was for $8 million to liquidate its assets.

In its nine-year history, the CCC had done an almost unbelievable amount of work. It had served its country well. Later generations are still reaping the benefits of its accomplishments.

Company commander, Capt. A.R. Morley (seated) and Sub-altern, Lt. Thomas Hay, reviewing the company records at the Gegoka Camp, Superior National Forest, Minnesota, 1940.
USFS

A supply depot at Fleet-wood, Pennsylvania, in March 1942. The CCC program was about to end due to wartime conditions and an enormous amount of supplies were coming into warehouses from the hundreds of camps throughout the country. A lot of the material was condemned, but some was reused in the war effort. NA

This CCC camp in Rupert, Idaho, was converted to wartime use. It was put under the control of the Farm Security Administration and used to house Japanese-American farm workers. LC

The unique character of the Chippewa National Forest log headquarters building at Cass Lake is immediately evident in observing its interesting structure. This building was constructed in 1935 of native red pine, logged from Star Island and Lake 13 areas. It was built in Finnish log construction style, by Finnish craftsmen, with the help of Civilian Conservation Corps and Work Project Administration laborers. This type of construction is considered to be a lost art, and perhaps would be impossible to duplicate today. This building, constructed entirely of Minnesota forest products, contains 8,500 square feet of floor space. More than 16,000 lineal feet of red pine logs 10 to 16 inches in diameter were used for outer walls and partitions. Birch, oak, maple and white pine were used as finishing materials. The building was erected under supervision of Ike Boekenoogen, a master woodsman. By March 1935, foundation work was done, and log work was started. Many of the logs were over 100 years old when cut. The logs are notched and grooved, requiring no chinking. Heavy wooden pegs hold many of the floor beams in place. Landscape work was in progress when the forest service moved into the building on April 8, 1936. Large trees were moved from the forest on specially designed sleds that would carry the huge balls of frozen dirt to protect the roots. The cost at the time of construction was approximately $225,000. Today this building stands as a monument to the pride and skill of the craftsmen who built it. Because of their knowledge and skill, this sturdy work of art, believed to be one of the largest log buildings in existence, should stand for many years to come. It was entered on the National Register of Historic Place on Jan. 31, 1976.

LEGACY
OF THE CCC

CHIPPEWA NATIONAL FOREST HEADQUARTERS

Construction photo 1935.

The 50-foot-high fireplace and chimney, which runs up through the air court in the center of the building, is very unusual. The fireplace is made of split and matched glacial boulders, native to this area, and is 14 by 14 feet at the base, tapering to 10 by 10 feet at its top. More than 265 tons of rock were used in its construction by Nels Bergler of Walker, Minnesota, its designer and builder.

The stairway railing was constructed by hand fitting selected maple trees and limbs that were damaged by frost. The frost contributed to the railing's gnarled appearance. The steps are built of split logs, hand-hewn with a broad axe, and planed smooth.

CAMP RABIDEAU – CHIPPEWA NATIONAL FOREST

Camp Rabideau is located six miles south of Blackduck, Minnesota, on County Road 39. Camp Rabideau is one of three remaining camps being preserved and was placed on the National Register of Historic Places in 1976. The camp's first enrollees, Company #3749 from Bennett Springs, Missouri, built and occupied the camp from August 1935 to Jan. 4, 1936. The crew was relocated in California and Minnesota Company #708 was moved from Bena to Camp Rabideau. Company #708 remained at Rabideau until the end of the program in 1941. Work projects ranged from building the Blackduck Ranger Station and two fire towers to doing deer census and searching for lost persons during the berry picking and deer hunting seasons. In 1945, the camp was leased to the University of Illinois for use by their engineering and forestry students. Under the terms of the lease, the students added sewer and sanitation lines, installed a water pressure system, rewired the buildings, installed ceiling supports and replaced the wood stoves with oil. After 27 years their lease ended in 1973. The camp is situated on a 112-acre tract purchased in 1934. The buildings sit about 100 feet apart, surrounded by tall trees forming a large glade in the center. The open area was once the location of the mess hall which burned down in the 1930s. Benjamin and Carls Lakes are visible from the barracks. An open air picnic shelter was built by the CCC and moved from the Cut Foot Sioux area to Camp Rabideau in 1986. Today, 15 of the original 25 buildings remain and four honor those who served as CCC corpsmen.

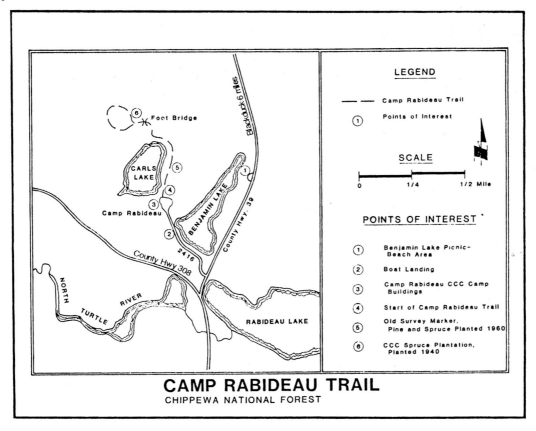

CAMP RABIDEAU TRAIL
CHIPPEWA NATIONAL FOREST

Camp Radideau
Today

Officers' barracks.

Forestry headquarters.

Mess hall.

Officers' quarters.

The Norway Beach Visitor Center, located 4 miles east of Cass Lake off U.S. Highway 2, Cass Lake Ranger District, Chippewa National Forest, Minnesota, offers Naturalist Programs throughout the summer. The log building constructed in 1936 stands as a tribute to the Civilian Conservation Corps workers who notched the logs and split the native stone to create this magnificent building.

Guernsey Museum building at Guernsey, Wyoming, built by the CCC. WYOMING STATE ARCHIVES

The ski lodge at Lookout Pass on the Montana-Idaho border was built by the CCC in 1941.

SHENANDOAH NATIONAL PARK

Buildings built by the CCC in Shenandoah National Park, Virginia. PHOTOS COURTESY SHENANDOAH NATIONAL PARK ARCHIVES

Barracks #3 at Pinnacles.

Maintenance building at Big Meadows.

Technical headquarters building at Camp Byrd NP-12.

La Purisima Mission near Lompoc, California, has a history dating back to the late 1700s. In 1812 an earthquake destroyed the mission and it was rebuilt in 1813, four miles from the original site. After abandonment in 1834, La Purisima slowly fell into total ruin. The decay was the result of neglect and weathering, particularly rain damage to the adobe walls. In 1934, through a combined effort of county, state and federal agencies, the restoration of La Purisima began. It was to become known as "The Best Restoration West of the Mississippi." Under the direction of the National Park Service, the Civilian Conservation Corps actually recreated the California of 1820. The site was dedicated as part of the State Park System on Dec. 7, 1941. Today La Purisima Mission State Historic Park is a popular tourist attraction.
LA PURISIMA MISSION STATE PARK
VIA RICK GROSSMAN

Bly fire lookout on the Bly Ranger District, Fremont National Forest, Oregon.
USFS

Leavenworth ski lodge at Leavenworth, Washington, on U.S. Highway 2, Wenatchee National Forest, built by the CCC. USFS

Glacier Ranger Station
Public Service Center,
Highway 542 East in the
Mt. Baker/Snoqualmie
National Forest,
Washington. USFS

Mt. Tamalpais State Park,
Marin Headlands, Califor-
nia, developed by the CCC.
STATE OF CALIFORNIA

Company #949, SP-7,
Summer Camp built
buildings, roads, trails and
shelters on Mount Spokane,
Washington. CCC crews dug
up rocks and hauled them
on stretchers to the site
where the Vista House was
built. It is now used by
Mount Spokane Ski Area.
USFS

Original CCC decal on the Camp Exchange window.

The old Thornwood CCC camp in northern Pocahontas County, West Virginia, is now the Monongahela National Forest Organization Camp and the site of the National Youth Science Camp (since 1963) and the county 4-H camp. The original barracks are still in use and the original camp exchange booth is still in place in the administration building. ROBERT KELER

The Wisconsin Chapter 23
of the NACCCA has
established a CCC museum
at Pioneer Park,
Rhinelander, Wisconsin.

CCC Company #1963, F-57
built this bridge which now
accesses the Squaw Creek
drainage area and Garnett
Mountain National Recrea-
tional Trail in the Gallatin
National Forest, Montana.
BILL SHARP

Fenn Ranger Station, the administrative center for the Selway Ranger District of the Nez Perce National Forest, was built during the years 1937-1940. Built at a cost that was staggering for the time, $500,000, the station was one of the most elaborate built by the Forest Service, and the attention to site design and building placement had not been seen in the Forest Service facilities prior to this. The extensive attention given to the design of the station can be attributed, at least in part, to the use of the Civilian Conservation Corps. Materials, stone and cedar, were procured locally. A quarry was located nearby, and split cedars for the roof were made at a mill near the station. The ranger station consists of 15 buildings, eight structures and two objects. It is on the National Register of Historic Places.

Painted Desert Inn on the Petrified Forest National Park in Arizona. The site overlooks the Painted Desert at Kachina Point two miles from the north entrance off I-40. The Inn is built in the Pueblo Revival style of architecture. The CCC built the building using an old house as its nucleus. Local Hispanic and Native Americans were recruited, mainly to work on interior furnishings. A large interior skylight inside depicts Hopi design elements. The Inn opened in 1940 after three years of construction and was operated for many years by the Fred Harvey chain. In 1948, Fred Kabotie, a noted Hopi artist, completed a series of wall murals which helped designate the building as a National Historic Landmark. After extensive remodeling the Inn reopened in 1991 as the park's visitor center.

The front of the Inn today, facing west.

Construction photo in the 1930s.

HISTORIC NINEMILE RANGER STATION, MONTANA

In 1930, the U.S. Forest Service established a re-mount depot to provide pack animals for fire and other emergency use. A site was picked in the Ninemile area near Alberton, Montana. In 1934-35, the CCC built the facility which was dedicated in 1936. The site is now on the National Register of Historic Places.

An early picture of the buildings at the Ninemile Remount Depot after their construction by the CCC. USFS

The Ninemile Remount Depot buildings were designed by Missoula, Montana, architect Bill Fox in a distinctive Cape Cod style. USFS

This barn is the centerpiece of the historic site. It housed animals as well as grain and equipment. Big draft mules lifted hay into the loft using a system of nets and pulleys. Hay was dropped from the loft into a manger. Today the barn is used to store equipment for all aspects of work on the Ninemile District.

Visitor's Center.

This dam and archbridge in Cumberland Mountain State Park, Crossville, Tennessee, is the largest masonry structure built by the CCC. Company #3464, SP-7, formerly NP-16, built this structure as well as a bathhouse and other facilities in the park. On Oct. 6, 1939, Sgt. Alvin York, WWI hero, was appointed Project Superintendent of CCC Co. 3464. ROGER THACKSTON, UNIVERSITY OF TENNESSEE, EXTENSION SERVICE

Visitor's Information Center, Devil's Den State Park, West Fork, Arkansas, is the most original intact CCC-built state park in Arkansas. CCC Companies 754, SP-6, 797, 3795 and SP-6 built the roads, 15 rental cabins, 10 miles of trails with stone steps and foot bridges, and a major portion of the landscaping.
ARKANSAS DEPT. OF PARKS AND TOURISM

This building stands as a monument to the young men of the CCC, partic- ularly Company #833, SP-1, who built it. This structure is the largest adobe office complex in the Unites States. It was completed in 1939 and is the headquarters of the National Park Service, Southwest Region, Santa Fe, New Mexico.
NATIONAL PARK SERVICE

Franklin D. Roosevelt State Park was built by CCC Company #4463, PS-13. This Company built this Inn, now the Park office, 11 cabins, roads, trails, two lakes, Lake Delano and Lake Franklin, a 50-meter Liberty Bell-shaped swimming pool, an amphitheater, stone bridge and entrance signs as well as landscaping and tree plantings. This 10,000-acre park is deeply rooted in the historical era of four-time U.S. President Franklin D. Roosevelt. Seeking a place for treatment after he was stricken with polio in 1921, Roosevelt traveled to Warm Springs and built The Little White House, now within the park boundary. TOURIST DIVISION GEORGIA DEPT. OF INDUSTRY & TRADE

Mother Neff State Park, Moody, Texas. The rustic stone structures built by CCC Company #817, SP-38, include an open-air pavilion, park residence and a water tower. The concession building is now the park headquarters. TEXAS PARKS & WILDLIFE DEPT.

This beautiful two-story Greek Revival home, The Gregory House, Torreya State Park, Florida, was originally located on the north side of the Apalachicola River. The home was abandoned and began to deteriorate. The home was totally dismantled by the CCC and moved approximately two miles from the flood plain to Neal's Bluff across the river where it was rebuilt by CCC Company #4453, SP-6. The CCC also built trails, bridges and roads in the park.

NACCCA

The NACCCA was established as a non-profit organization in August 1977. Articles of Incorporation were filed with the California Secretary of State on Aug. 16, 1977. National headquarters was subsequently moved from Sacramento, California, to Virginia, in 1980 and to St. Louis, Missouri, in 1986.

Now located in a turn-of-the-century building at 16 Hancock Ave. (pictured above) in Jefferson Barracks Historical Park, in suburban St. Louis, the NACCCA Museum and Library contains more than 100,000 photographs, papers and other memorabilia from the CCC.

Jefferson Barracks, then an active Army post, was an induction and conditioning center for the CCC. Thousands of young men spent time there getting into shape for their service in wilderness and rural areas in the Midwest.

The exhibits show how the men worked, the tools they used and living conditions in camps from across the country. It is also the national headquarters for the nationwide alumni organization. Museum hours generally are 9 a.m. to 3 p.m. Monday through Thursday; until 1 p.m. on Friday. It is closed on weekends. Like most Park buildings, it is on the National Register of Historic Places.

Membership is open to all who served, in any capacity, with the original CCC. In order to perpetuate the CCC history and philosophy, membership has been extended to those who have served in less extensive modern-day CCC-like programs such as the Young Adult Conservation Corps (YACC), the Youth Conservation Corps (YCC) plus the California Conservation Corps and other state CCC programs now or soon to be underway.

NACCCA also operates a website— www.cccalumni.org— which has extensive information on the history of the CCC and the location of over 4,800 camps throughout the United States. The website also details how CCCers and descendants can obtain copies of discharge papers and gives guidelines for seeking research assistance from NACCCA staff and volunteers.

NACCCA can be contacted by writing: PO Box 16429, St. Louis, MO 63125. Phone: (314) 487-8666; FAX (314) 487-9488.

THE CALIFORNIA CONSERVATION CORPS
"Hard work, low pay, miserable conditions"

The California Conservation Corps, which shares the same initials as the Civilian Conservation Corps, was established in 1976. Modeled after the original CCC, the California program has always pursued a dual mission: the employment and development of young people, and the protection and enhancement of the state's environmental resources. It is a work ethic program stressing service and education.

In California, most of the state parks were built by the original CCC. More than fifty years later, today's corpsmembers work in many of the same locations. Corpsmembers also provide restoration work at historic California sites, including missions, that were originally restored by the Civilian Conservation Corps. Today's CCC tackles a wide range of conservation projects in both rural and urban areas throughout California.

Along with the day-to-day natural resource work, the members of the California Conservation Corps follow in the footsteps of the original CCC enrollees in providing assistance following natural disasters. Corpsmembers fight fires, floods, oil spills, earthquakes, and agricultural pest infestations, and have developed a reputation as one of the state's premier emergency response forces.

Each year, California's CCC hires more than 1,800 corpsmembers throughout the state. Today's Corps hires both men and women, with the main requirement being that they be between the ages of 18 and 23. Since the program was established, more than 50,000 young people have participated in the California Conservation Corps.

The oldest and largest program of its kind in the country, the California Conservation Corps is looked to as a model for state and local corps and for youth service programs in general.

Other states that have instituted a statewide conservation corps program include: Arizona, Arkansas, Florida, Georgia, Iowa, Maryland, Minnesota, Montana, New Hampshire, New Jersey, Ohio, Oregon, Pennsylvania, Washington, West Virginia and Wisconsin. Many local programs have been started throughout the country including summer projects in New York, Maine and Vermont. Other programs include The Student Conservation Association, USDA Forest Service Youth Conservation Corps and Youth Volunteer Corps of America.

COURTESY NATIONAL ASSOCIATION OF SERVICE & CONSERVATION CORPS, WASHINGTON, D.C.

APPENDIX

The Civilian Conservation Corps made an outstanding record in the conservation of human and natural resources. Jobs, health, and work training were given to about 3,000,000 young men, including war veterans, Indians, and territorials. The CCC advanced natural resource conservation in such fields as reforestation and erosion control by from twenty-five to thirty-five years, completing work on an estimated present and potential value of more than $1,750,000,000. In addition to training idle young men and advancing conservation, the CCC demonstrated its great usefulness as a training and national preparedness agency. Graduates of the CCC made splendid soldier material and excellent war production workers. The work that they completed materially strengthened the nation economically.*

The following statistics are taken from the final CCC report in 1942.

Total enrollments (some individuals enrolled more than once)—3,465,766.

Juniors, veterans, and Indian enrollees—2,876,638

Territorial enrollees (estimated)—50,000

Nonenrolled personnel (camp officers, work supervisors, educational advisors, etc.)—263,755

Average number of barrack camps operating in the United States per year—1,643

Total number of different camps, 1933-1942—4,500

Total obligations (estimated) (includes obligations for food, shelter, construction of camps, transportation, personal services)—$2,969,000,000

Allotments to dependents by enrollees (estimated)—$662,895,000

Each state had a CCC program during the nine-year history of the Corps. Men worked either in their own state or were transferred to an out-of-state camp. The following is a brief summation of work accomplished, number of enrollees from within and without the state, number of camps, and total financial obligations.*

ALABAMA: Major work was carried out in forest and soil resources. The CCC was the major forest-patrolling and fire-fighting force in the state. Many parks, bridges, erosion dams and roads were built. Major historical work was accomplished at Mound State Park. Over 66,000 Alabama men from the state were enrolled. An average of 30 camps a year were operated with a total financial obligation within the state of more than $55,000,000.

ARIZONA: Major work consisted of the improvements in forest and grazing areas. Water and soil erosion projects were built in the arid and semi-arid grazing lands. Park development and insect and disease control were also important. Much work was done on the Indian reservations. Over 41,000 men from the state were enrolled and more than 52,000 men served in the state. An average of 31 camps a year were operated with a total financial obligation within the state of more than $58,000,000.

ARKANSAS: Major works accomplished were the improvement and protection of the state's forests and the control of erosion on farm lands. Recreational facilities were built and wildlife conditions were improved. Over 75,000 men from the state were enrolled and more than 62,000 men served in the state. An average of 37 camps a year were operated with a total financial obligation within the state of more than $64,000,000.

CALIFORNIA: The state was one of the largest benefactors of CCC programs. Forest improvements and protection were the main projects accomplished. Park development, both local and national, were great along with soil erosion control projects and historical restorations. Over 135,000 men from the state were enrolled and more than 166,000 men served in the state. An average of 98 camps a year were operated with a total financial obligation within the state of more than $154,500,000.

COLORADO: Fire fighting, reforestation, and soil erosion control projects were the major accomplishments. Irrigation facilities were cleaned and improved. Grazing control operations restored grass and water to vast stretches of land for cattle and sheep grazing and opened new areas for use. Over 35,000 men from the state were enrolled and more than 57,000 men served in the state. An average of 34 camps a year were operated with a total financial obligation within the state of more than $63,700,000.

CONNECTICUT: Major work projects were in timber stand improvement, forest insect control, and development of recreational facilities. The Corps was an important factor in cleaning up the tremendous damage caused by the hurricane of September 1938. More than

---

*Final Report of the CCC by Director James J. McEntee in 1942.

*Excerpted from Final Report of the CCC by Director James J. McEntee, 1942.

30,600 men from the state were enrolled and more than 22,000 men served in the state. An average of 13 camps a year were operated with a total financial obligation within the state of more than $20,700,000.

DELAWARE: Mosquito control operations along the salt marshes of the ocean shore were a major work accomplishment along with the clearing and maintenance of over 12 million yards of drainage and flood control ditches. More than 5,300 men from the state were enrolled and more than 6,700 men served in the state. An average of four camps a year were operated with a total financial obligation within the state of more than $8,300,00.

DISTRICT OF COLUMBIA: Major park development was accomplished at Rock Creek Park and development of the National Arboretum was greatly accelerated. More than 11,400 men from the district were enrolled. An average of two camps a year were operated with a total financial obligation within the district of more than $4,300,000.

FLORIDA: Enrollees reforested wastelands, developed new recreational facilities, aided in the control of erosion on farms, and improved conditions for wildlife. More than 49,000 men from the state were enrolled. An average of 21 camps were operated with a total financial obligation within the state of more than $34,200,000.

GEORGIA: Reforestation of wastelands and erosion control in agricultural areas was the major work performed. Restoration of historical sites, such as Fort Pulaski and Kenesaw Mountain, and archeological excavations helped establish an extensive statewide park system. The Corps also developed the Okefenokee Wildlife Refuge. More than 78,600 men from the state were enrolled. An average of 35 camps a year were operated with a total financial obligation within the state of more than $69,500,000.

IDAHO: The protection from fire, insects, and blister rust disease in the state's forests was the greatest achievement of the CCC. Forest areas were improved by thinning trees and planting millions of seedlings. Soil erosion control and water reclamation control in the southern part of the state were also beneficial. More than 28,000 men from the state were enrolled and more than 37,700 men served in the state. An average of 51 camps a year were operated with a total financial obligation within the state of more than $82,000,000.

ILLINOIS: Improvement of the state's natural resources and recreational facilities was the major benefit. Chicago received a major share of the new recreational construction, especially in the development of the Skokie Lagoons of the Cook County forest preserve. More than 165,300 men from the state were enrolled and more than 92,000 men served in the state. An average of 54 camps a year were operated with a total financial obligation within the state of more than $103,600,000.

INDIANA: The CCC effected extensive improvements on the state's agricultural lands through the construction of check dams, bank sloping, terracing of fields, strip cropping, and the planting of trees and other vegetation on gullied areas. A large improvement in the state park system was undertaken. More than 63,700 men from the state were enrolled. An average of 30 camps a year were operated with a total financial obligation within the state of more than $55,300,000.

IOWA: Erosion control on the state's rich agricultural lands was the main benefit of the CCC. The state's park and forest areas were also developed. Recreational facilities were built throughout the state. More than 45,800 men from the state were enrolled and more than 49,200 men served in the state. An average of 29 camps a year were operated with a total financial obligation within the state of more than $48,400,000.

KANSAS: Drought conditions and massive soil erosion was alleviated by CCC work. Land was prepared for strip cropping and contour furrows and terraces were installed to prevent sheet erosion. Many impounding and diversion dams were built to conserve water. More than 38,000 men from the state were enrolled. An average of 15 camps a year were operated with a total financial obligation within the state of more than $32,600,000.

KENTUCKY: Reforestation, soil erosion control of the state's farmlands, and the improvements in the state's park system were the major accomplishments. Outstanding work was done at Mammoth Cave National Park and in the Cumberland National Forest. More than 89,500 men from the state were enrolled. An average of 33 camps a year were operated with a total financial obligation within the state of more than $62,200,000.

LOUISIANA: Tree planting, fire protection, and timber stand improvements of the state's forests were major jobs accomplished. Soil binding grass and shrubs were planted, dams built, and water channels cleared for extensive flood control projects. The Sabine Migratory Waterfowl Refuge was developed. Many enrollees were engaged in hurricane and flood relief work. More than

51,800 men from the state were enrolled and more than 51,200 men served in the state. An average of 30 camps a year were operated with a total financial obligation within the state of more than $55,800,000.

MAINE: Work was concentrated largely on reforestation and forest protection activities. Many recreational facilities such as buildings, camp grounds, road and foot trails were constructed in national, state, and private forests. More than 18,200 men from the state were enrolled and more than 20,400 men served in the state. An average of 12 camps a year were operated with a total financial obligation within the state of more than $18,500,000.

MARYLAND: Intense management was conducted on Maryland's forests and recreational facilities. Although the number of acres of farm land in the state was not large, much soil erosion work was completed. More than 32,800 men from the state were enrolled and more than 35,800 served in the state. An average of 21 camps a year were operated with a total financial obligation within the state of more than $39,700,000.

MASSACHUSETTS: Tree planting, fire fighting, and tree and plant disease and insect control were the main work accomplishments. Many recreational facilities were built in the forests and parks including the construction of facilities for winter sports. Exceptionally valuable work was done by the Corps after the 1938 hurricane. More than 99,500 men from the state were enrolled. An average of 28 camps a year were operated with a total financial obligation within the state of more than $45,100,000.

MICHIGAN: Tree planting was the major reforestation project completed. More than 485 million seedlings were planted. Fire fighting, timber stand improvement, and disease and insect control were major accomplishments. Recreational and wildlife facilities were built along with the stocking of millions of fish in the state's lakes and streams. More than 102,000 men from the state were enrolled and more than 97,000 men served in the state. An average of 57 camps a year were operated with a total financial obligation within the state of more than $84,900,000.

MINNESOTA: Tree planting on the state's vast forest land was a major accomplishment along with fire fighting, lookout tower construction, and recreational development. Millions of fish were stocked in the thousands of state lakes. More than 84,000 men from the state were enrolled and more than 86,700 men served in the state. An average of 51 camps a year were operated with

a total financial obligation within the state of more than $84,900,000.

MISSISSIPPI: Improvement and protection of the state's timber and inauguration of soil conservation practices on its rich farmlands were the two major accomplishments. Wildlife and recreational facilities were constructed. Flood control projects and flood relief work were also carried out. More than 57,900 men from the state were enrolled and more than 56,200 men served in the state. An average of 33 camps a year were operated with a total financial obligation within the state of more than $60,900,000.

MISSOURI: Soil conservation work including reforestation, gully bank sloping, seeding eroded lands, and terracing were major accomplishments. Several national and state parks were developed. Important wildlife conservation work was carried out at Swan Lake Wildlife Refuge. More than 102,000 men from the state were enrolled. An average of 41 camps a year were operated with a total financial obligation within the state of more than $71,900,000.

MONTANA: Forestry projects in the timbered areas of the western part of the state were of great importance and soil erosion work in the eastern part of the state stabilized soil problems there. Extensive work was done at Glacier National Park and other state parks, and a major migratory wildlife refuge was built at Medicine Lake. More than 25,600 men from the state were enrolled and more than 40,800 men served in the state. An average of 24 camps a year were operated with a total financial obligation within the state of more than $42,300,000.

NEBRASKA: Erosion control by tree planting, terrace construction, building check dams and diversion ditches were the major accomplishments. Expansion of nursery and planting work on the Nebraska National Forest along with the development of wildlife facilities were also accomplished. More than 30,700 men from the state were enrolled. An average of 16 camps a year were operated within the state with a total financial obligation of more than $34,200,000.

NEVADA: Most of the projects were on the vast grazing lands. More than a thousand miles of fence were built to control stock movements on the ranges. Springs and waterholes were cleaned, check dams and water control structures were built, and large rodent and predatory animal control projects were initiated. More than 7,000 men from the state were enrolled and more than 30,700 men served in the state. An average of 18 camps a year were operated with a total financial obligation within the state of more than $31,900,000.

NEW HAMPSHIRE: Most of the projects concentrated on reforestation, forest protection, and park development. The CCC played a major part in the rescue and cleanup work following the 1938 New England hurricane. The Corps also performed valuable work in controlling forest losses caused by the gypsy moth and white pine blister rust. More than 10,600 men from the state were enrolled and more than 22,000 served in the state. An average of 13 camps a year were operated with a total financial obligation within the state of more than $21,700,000.

NEW JERSEY: State forests and parks were developed for public use by the construction of cabins, shelters, bridges, dams, picnic areas and outdoor fireplaces. Reforestation, fire prevention and soil erosion work was also done. The CCC built a fish hatchery and the Brigantine Migratory Waterfowl Refuge. More than 91,500 men from the state were enrolled. An average of 25 camps a year were operated with a total financial obligation within the state of more than $46,700,000.

NEW MEXICO: Reforestation and soil erosion projects were the major jobs accomplished. Extensive work was done in road building, laying of telephone lines, building of small dams and the development of springs and small reservoirs. Rodent and predatory animal control programs were successfully implemented. An outstanding project was the construction of the Elephant Butte Fish Hatchery. Much work was done on Indian reservations. More than 32,300 men from the state were enrolled and more than 54,500 men served in the state. An average of 32 camps a year were operated with a total financial obligation within the state of more than $63,370,000.

NEW YORK: Reforestation and the improvement of forest and park areas throughout the state were the major accomplishments. Tree disease and insect pest control projects were initiated. More than 220,700 men from the state were enrolled, the greatest number of any of the states. An average of 68 camps a year were operated with a total financial obligation within the state of over $134,500,000.

NORTH CAROLINA: Reforestation and soil erosion projects, including tree planting, fire fighting, timber stand improvement, and gully erosion control were accomplished. Recreational facilities were also built. More than 75,800 men from the state were enrolled and more than 76,600 men served in the state. An average of 45 camps a year were operated with a total financial obliga-

tion within the state of more than $82,300,000.

NORTH DAKOTA: Water conservation, erosion control on farm lands, improvement of conditions for wildlife, and park development were the major projects. Major work was accomplished on Indian reservations. The waterfowl refuges on the Des Lacs and Upper and Lower Soceris Rivers were developed. More than 31,700 men from the state were enrolled. An average of eight camps a year were operated with a total financial obligation within the state of more than $16,200,000.

OHIO: Work consisted of the rehabilitation of drainage ditches, development of state parks, reforestation, erosion control demonstrations on farm lands, construction of check dams, and parkway construction. Enrollees helped in rescue and flood control during the 1937 Ohio-Mississippi River flood. More than 139,400 men from the state were enrolled. An average of 33 camps a year were operated with a total financial obligation within the state of more than 61,900,000.

OKLAHOMA: Soil erosion projects on the state's farm lands and Indian reservations were the main work projects. Other projects included the establishment of a number of state parks and the improvement and protection of forest areas and conditions for wildlife. More than 107,600 men from the state, 21,300 of them Indians, were enrolled. An average of 33 camps a year were operated with a total financial obligation within the state of more than $63,800,000.

OREGON: Fire fighting and timber improvement were the major projects in the western part of the state. In the eastern part, grazing areas were improved and irrigation systems were cleaned and restored. Campgrounds were built and the Malhour and Hart Mountain Wildlife Refuges were developed. More than 34,600 men from the state were enrolled and more than 86,700 men served in the state. An average of 51 camps a year were operated with a total financial obligation within the state of more than $87,700,000.

PENNSYLVANIA: Extensive work was done in the state's forests with reforestation and fire control and on the state's farm lands with erosion control. Many major parks were reconstructed or established. Historical restorations were carried on at Fort Necessity, Gettysburg and other sites. More than 194,500 men from the state were enrolled. An average of 74 camps a year were operated with a total financial obligation within the state of more than $126,400,000.

RHODE ISLAND: Major activities included emergency

work after the 1938 New England hurricane and the protection of timber against fire, forest insects and disease. More than 15,900 men from the state were enrolled. An average of four camps a year were operated with a financial obligation within the state of more than $8,800,0000.

SOUTH CAROLINA: Major work included erosion control on private farm lands, forest protection, state park development and improvement of wildlife areas. One of the most important links in the Atlantic seaboard chain of migratory waterfowl refuges was developed with the aid of the Corps. More than 48,100 men from the state were enrolled and more than 49,200 men served in the state. An average of 29 camps a year were operated with a total financial obligation within the state of more than $57,100,000.

SOUTH DAKOTA: Extensive work was done on fire protection, reforestation and developing recreational facilities in the Harney and Black Hills National Forests. Water control dams were built. The CCC developed Wind Cave National Park, Custer State Park and Badlands National Monument. More than 31,000 men from the state were enrolled and more than 32,400 men served in the state. An average of 19 camps a year were operated with a total financial obligation within the state of more than $30,400,000.

TENNESSEE: Reforestation, fire fighting and soil erosion projects were the major work accomplishments. The Tennessee Valley Authority camps worked on fire fighting and tree planting. The state park system was developed by the CCC. More than 72,600 men from the state were enrolled and more than 76,600 men served in the state. An average of 45 camps a year were operated with a total financial obligation within the state of more than $71,900,00.

TEXAS: Work projects included developing a state park system, protecting farms from soil erosion and developing new forest areas. More than 6,000 miles of truck trails and roads were built. More than 156,400 men from the state were enrolled. An average of 58 camps per year were operated with a total financial obligation within the state of more than $110,600,000.

UTAH: Projects included the improvement of grazing conditions on rangeland, water conservation, control of rodent and predatory animals, erosion control and forest protection. Hundreds of miles of fences and guard rails were constructed along with large water diversion dams. More than 22,000 men from the state were enrolled and more than 45,900 men served in the state.

An average of 27 camps per year were operated with a total financial obligation within the state of more than $52,700,000.

VERMONT: Flood control and tree insect pest control were two important projects. Flood detention dams were erected above Barre, Montpelier and Waterbury in the Winooski River Valley, greatly reducing the flood potential in the area. Many types of forestry and recreational projects were completed. More than 11,200 men from the state were enrolled and more than 40,800 men served in the state. An average of 24 camps a year were operated with a total financial obligation within the state of more than $40,500,000.

VIRGINIA: Major jobs were instituted in the state's national and state forests in reforestation, fire protection and recreation. The state park system was greatly improved by the Corps. Historical areas such as Jamestown, Williamsburg, Yorktown, Fredericksburg and Spotsylvania were developed. More than 75,100 men from the state were enrolled and more than 107,00 men served in the state. An average of 63 camps a year were operated with a total financial obligation within the state of more than $108,900,000.

WASHINGTON: Important work was done in the state's vast timber areas. Reforestation, fire fighting, blister rust and pest control and recreational development work was performed. Soil erosion control work was done in the eastern part of the state. More than 51,300 men from the state were enrolled and more than 73,300 men served in the state. An average of 43 camps a year were operated with a total financial obligation within the state of more than $76,600,000.

WEST VIRGINIA: Work programs included the development of a state park system and important work in forest protection and improvement in the Monongahela National Forest. Soil conservation work was done on the state's farmlands. More than 55,000 men from the state were enrolled. An average of 26 camps a year were operated with a total financial obligation within the state of more than $50,200,000.

WISCONSIN: Forest protection and tree planting were the outstanding achievements. Recreational facilities were greatly improved and millions of fish were stocked in the streams and lakes in the state. More than 75,200 men from the state were enrolled and more than 92,000 men served in the state. An average of 54 camps a year were operated with a total financial obligation within the state of more than $96,500,000.

WYOMING: Forest protection, grazing control and water conservation projects were instituted. Rebuilding of irrigation systems and constructing earth reservoirs developed water supplies for agriculture. Many winter and summer recreational facilities were built. One camp was engaged continually in controlling coal bed fires near Gillette. More than 12,800 men from the state were enrolled and more than 36,100 men served in the state. An average of 21 camps were operated with a total financial obligation within the state of more than $38,500,000.

A magazine published by the Fort Missoula district of the CCC, Missoula, Montana, 1937.

The CCC increased business opportunities for supplying material throughout the country as is shown by this ad.

C-42
Sergt. Chevron

C-43
Corp. Chevron

C-44
Leader

C-45
Asst. Leader

C-46
Foreman

C-47
Steward

C-48
Storekeeper

C-49
Truck

C-50
Laborer

C-51
1st Aid
Hospital Corps

C-1

C-3

SLEEVE AND CAP
EMBLEMS

C-54
Co. Numerals

C-4
Cap and Collar
Disc

C-52
Clerk

C-53
Cook

C-2
Re-enlistment
Service Stripes

SPORTSWEAR EMBLEMS

C-11
Silk Handkerchief

C-24

C-37

C-25

Please do not cut illustrations. Order by number

INSIGNIA AND SPECIAL ORNAMENTS

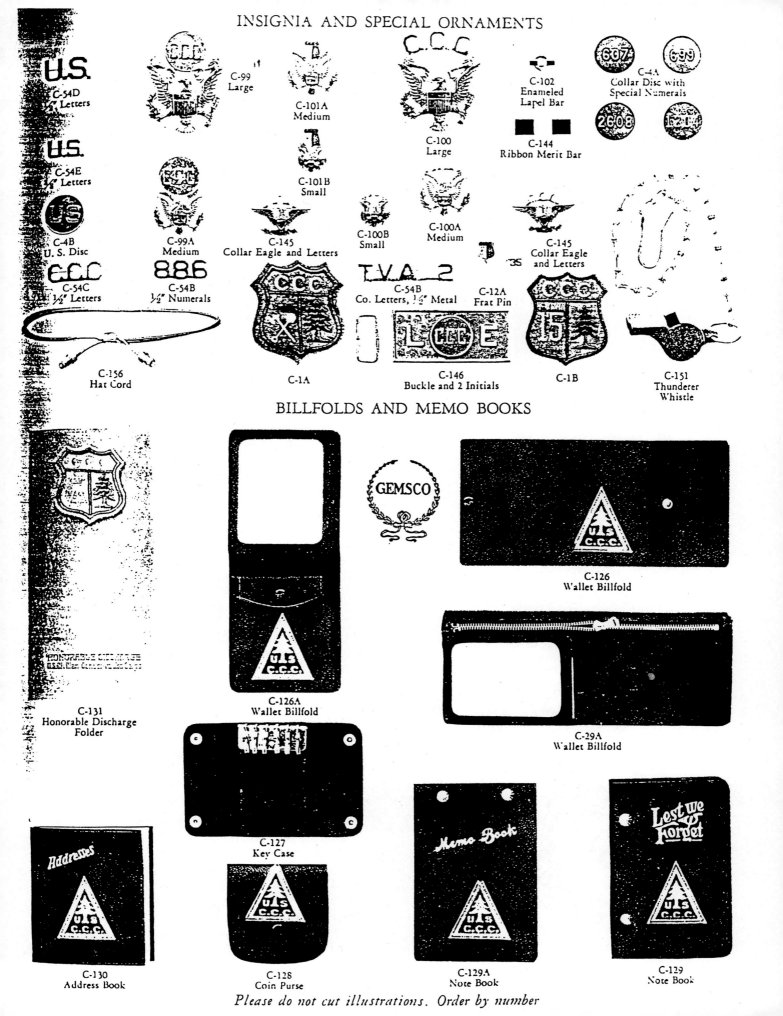

U.S.
C-54D
¾" Letters

U.S.
C-54E
⅜" Letters

C-99
Large

C-101A
Medium

C.C.C
C-100
Large

C-102
Enameled
Lapel Bar

607   699
C-4A
Collar Disc with
Special Numerals

2608   1211

C-4B
U. S. Disc

C-99A
Medium

C-101B
Small

C-145
Collar Eagle and Letters

C-100B
Small

C-100A
Medium

C-145
Collar Eagle
and Letters

C.C.C
C-54C
½" Letters

886
C-54B
½" Numerals

T.V.A. 2
C-54B
Co. Letters, ½" Metal

C-12A
Frat Pin

C-144
Ribbon Merit Bar

C-156
Hat Cord

C-1A

C-146
Buckle and 2 Initials

C-1B

C-151
Thunderer
Whistle

BILLFOLDS AND MEMO BOOKS

C-131
Honorable Discharge
Folder

C-126A
Wallet Billfold

GEMSCO

C-126
Wallet Billfold

C-29A
Wallet Billfold

C-127
Key Case

C-130
Address Book

C-128
Coin Purse

C-129A
Note Book

C-129
Note Book

Please do not cut illustrations. Order by number

GEMSCO

C-142A

C-143B

C-24A   C-24B

C-34
Tie

C-137A
Tie

C-140
Pillow Top

C-141
Beret

C-141A
Beret

C-141B
Beret

C-155B
Pennant

C-155A
Pennant

C-154
Guidon

Please do not cut illustrations. Order by number

Gemsco

MANUFACTURERS
DISTRIBUTORS

New York, N. Y.

SMOKERS
ARTICLES

TOBACCO
POUCHES
PIPES
CIGARETTE
CASES
LIGHTERS

GEMSCO

C-84 Tobacco Pouch
& Pipe Holder

C-82 Tobacco Pouch

C-81 Tobacco Pouch

C-133 Tobacco Pouch

C-83 Tobacco Pouch
& Pipe Holder

C-90A Yello Bowl

C-90B Yello Bowl

C-90C Yello Bowl

C-87A
Rocky Briar

C-87B
Rocky Briar

C-87C
Rocky Briar

C-88
Leather Cigarette Case

C-89
Zipper Leather
Cigarette Case

C-86
Cigarette Case

C-91 Combination
Cigarette Case
and Lighter Set

C-93
Tiny Pocket Lighter

C-92
Jumbo Table Lighter

C-85
Inco Storm Lighter

C-94
Table Lighter

Please do not cut illustrations.   Order by number

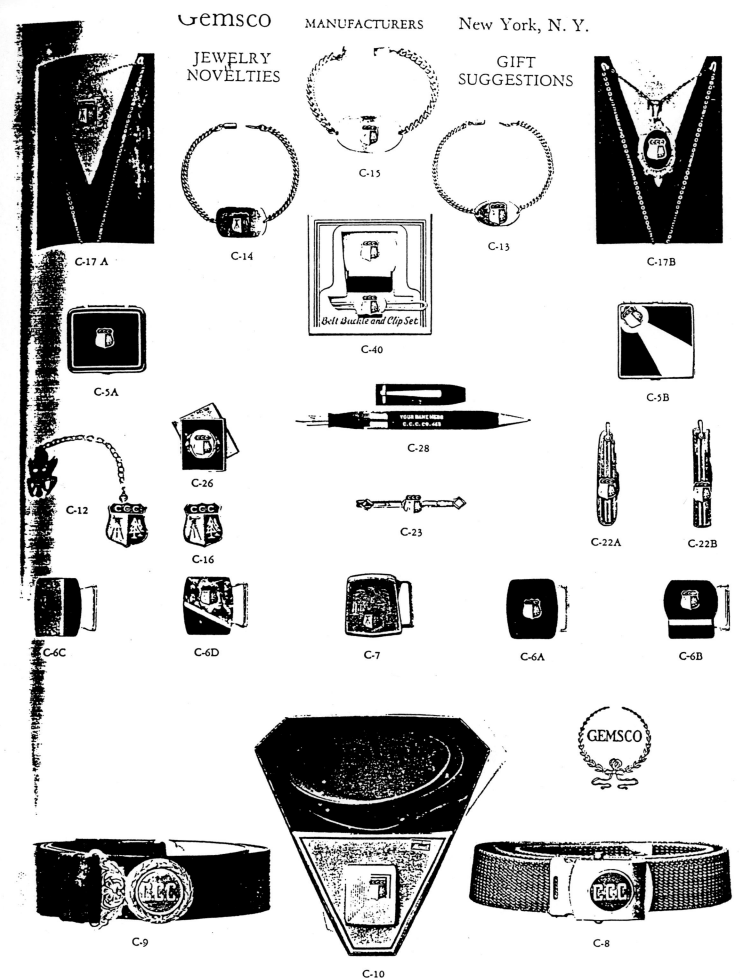

Gemsco MANUFACTURERS New York, N.Y.

JEWELRY NOVELTIES

GIFT SUGGESTIONS

C-17 A

C-14

C-15

C-13

C-17B

C-5A

Belt Buckle and Clip Set
C-40

C-5B

C-26

C-28

C-22A   C-22B

C-12

C-16

C-23

C-6C

C-6D

C-7

C-6A

C-6B

GEMSCO

C-9

C-10

C-8

Please do not cut illustrations. Order by number

MANUFACTURERS   New York, N. Y.

JEWELRY
NOVELTIES

GIFT
SUGGESTIONS

C-23B

C-23A

C-57

C-57

C-17D
Lavaliere

C-17C
Lavaliere

VANITY CASES (COMPACTS)

C-96A

C-95A

C-95B

C-95

C-96

C-135

C-135A

C-135B

C-135C

C-138
Tie
Guide

C-97A

C-97B

C-97C

C-136
Cigarette Case

C-135D Compact and Cigarette Case

C-135D Open View

C-137
Tie

C-136A
Cigarette Case

RINGS

C-39
Tie Holder Clip

C-139A
Collar Holder and
Tie Clip Set

C-26

C-27

C-98A

C-98

C-139B
Collar Holder and
Tie Clip Set

Please do not cut illustrations. Order by number

PILLOW TOPS
12½" x 15½"

C-20 Mother

SCRAP BOOK

SCRAPS

C-35

PILLOW TOPS
12½" x 15½"

C-20 Sweetheart

PHOTO ALBUM

HAPPY DAYS C.C.C.

C-19

MEMORY ALBUM

C-18

C-20 Sister

C-20 Friend

AUTOGRAPH ALBUM

BUDDIES of MINE

C-36

BILLFOLD

C-29

PASS CASE

C-41

C-20 Think of Me

C-20 Father

Please do not cut illustrations. Order by number

Enrollee Ernest Clark from Ozark, Arkansas, at the Luna Lake Camp, Superior National Forest, Minnesota, 1940. USFS

THE CCC — A YOUNG MAN'S OPPORTUNITY

to work

to live
to learn
to build

— and to conserve our National Resources

SHENANDOAH NATIONAL PARK
AND THE SKYLINE DRIVE

The park and drive are located in the western area of Virginia.

In May 1926, President Calvin Coolidge signed a bill authorizing the creation of Shenandoah National Park, however it was not until July 3, 1936, that the land was officially dedicated by President Roosevelt.

Construction of the Skyline Drive began in 1931 at Skyland, progressing south to Swift Run Gap over the next few years until it opened to traffic in 1934. The drive was built by private contractors, hiring drought-stricken farmers for the initial construction. CCC labor was used for the landscaping after the drive became part of the newly established park in late 1935.

President Roosevelt wanted to place the first CCC camp, in the spring of 1933, in the park but there was no staff or camp sites ready for the first enrollees. Therefore, the first camp was established in the nearby George Washington National Forest near Edinburg, Virginia.

CCC camps were placed in the park at Skyland (NP-1); Big Meadows (NP-2); beside Skyline Drive, north of Swift Run Gap (NP-3); near Front Royal (NP-4); Grottoes (NP-5); and Sperryville (NP-6). In addition camps NP-10, NP-12, NP-26 and NP-27 were placed in the park.

In August 1933, President Roosevelt visited the park. A local newspaper reported:

Saturday was the day of days in the history of the civilian conservation camps at Big Meadows...when President Franklin Delano Roosevelt and three members of his cabinet sat down with the boys for dinner and ate out of the regulation aluminum mess kit, consisting of a plate, cup containing about a pint, and knife, fork and spoon. It was a thoroughly democratic function for eight of the rank and file members of the camp were honored with a seat at the President's table, which was set on the blue grass on the edge of the camp while the remainder of the visitors and the camp personnel were eating in the mess hall. At the right of the President sat Secretary of the Interior Ickes and Gen. Malone, area commanding officer of the camps. To Mr. Roosevelt's left sat Secretary of Agriculture Wallace and Secretary of War Dern...

The CCC continued to work in the park and on the drive until the organization was disbanded in 1942 due to wartime priorities. They had worked on one of the most popular recreational areas in the east and restored it for use by the public decades into the future.

E. Ray Schaffner, a former Chief of Interpretation of the park, stands in front of a CCC sign.

SHENANDOAH NATIONAL PARK

Each day a retreat was held before the evening meal. Enrollees were given a job, adequate food, some vocational and educational training, and a sense of comraderie and respect for flag and country. PHOTOS COURTESY SHENANDOAH NATIONAL PARK ARCHIVES

Camp NP-3 street scene in the grip of winter, 1934-35.

Work crews build a guard rail and grade banks on Skyline Drive, which bisects the park.

Monument built by enrollees at a park camp to honor President Roosevelt.

Large, balled, bracted balsam fir trees were dug up in the park and transplanted to other sites.

The camp exchange provided modest "goodies" on credit each month, paid for out of the $5 a month each enrollee could keep of his paycheck. The other $25 was sent home to his family.

A fire lookout built by CCC enrollees.

Enrollees from Camp NP-12 practice raking a fire line.

Barracks at Camp NP-3. The "chunk" stove burned blighted chestnut trees found in the area.

THE FLAGPOLE NEWS

Vol.IV,No.II   Camp Skyland,Friday,Feb. 24,1939   Covers the Mountaintop

SAMUELS ACCEPTS DISCHARGE
-o-   -o-

Prominent Stanardsville Man With Corps Almost Two Years
-*-   -*-

Hq.Feb.20::Having served in the Corps for almost two years following his enlistment in April,1937, Jake L.Samuels of Stanardsville,accepted a discharge here today.

This is a continuation of the police of thos members who would have to leave in March getting out and getting employment before the spring rush for jobs,caused by the estimated hundred thousand who will have to leave at that time.

PROFESSOR'S SHOES HARD TO FILL
-*-   -*-

Stromitis will Resign when Successor is Found
--   --   --

Kitchen,Feb.23::Mess Steward George H.Gray is looking for a Wood & Water man. Ever since the discharge of Harry (Professor) Schuler of Baltimore on Feb. 2nd, he has found it difficult to fill this important post on his staff. Dodi Thompson of Altoona,Pa. accepted the job when Professor left,relinquished it a few days later to Leonard (Frankenstein) Stromitis of Shamokin,Pa. On Feb.16, Frankenstein announced his intention of resigning,was persuaded to remain on the job until a satisfactory successor could be located. The job is open to almost anyone at the present.

Stromitis gave as his reason for wishing to be relieved of the job that he "didn't understand just what the job consisted of when he accepted the appointment.

BLUE DEVILS WANT ANOTHER CHANCE AT STANLEY HIGH, EX-MANAGER ANNOUNCES
..   ..

Feel Confident of Victory in Second Trial
**   **   **

Hq.Feb.20::Smarting under a 29-22 defeat administered by the Stanley High School in Stanley on Jan.14th, the Blue Devils announced here tonight that they were out to get another try at the crack Stanley Team. Speaking for the team,Joseph J. Harvey, former manager,said,"I wish to convey to Lieut. Holdsworth the demands of the camp. It seems the boys still think that our team can beat the Stanley Team.".

Camp officials,meanwhile,are quietly investigating the rumor that the movement was fermented by Bronck E.Zaboy, timekeeper at the last Stanley-Skyland game. He is alleged to have held hands with an attractive young lady during the game.

Robert C.Trumbore, star player,is also said to have lost more than the game that night--his heart being that something. He denies the rumor, however.

JOSEPH W. HARVEY ACCEPTS FIRST AID JOB
-*-   -*-

Back on Overhead after Four Months
-oOo-   -oOo-

Hosp,Feb.20::In a surprise move, Joseph W.Harvey announced here early today that he had accepted appointment to the overhead position of First Aid Assistant in charge of the hospital. He took over his new duties here today. Irving Theilig,serving in the position temporarily following the unexpected resignation of "Dr." Henry Majoski earlier this month, will go back to private life on the road. Dr.Harvey's move was entirely unpredicted; especially since he had vowed never again to serve on the overhead following his resignation from the position of Post Exchange Steward last November.Dr. Harvey also served as Company Clerk for a period of several months last year.

Pressed for an explanation by reporters, Harvey stated that he had changed his mind about leaving the Corps in March,had accepted the position only after "much thoughtful consideration".

ThePOW-WOW

Season's Greetings

Published by The Fechner Indians
350th. Co. CCC - SNP-2 - Luray, Virginia
Vol. I ~ November 1935 ~ No. 8

5th CAEd. Form 2A

EDUCATIONAL AND VOCATIONAL RECORD OF DISCHARGED CCC ENROLLEES

CCC Company 3527 Camp S-75 Located at Morgantown, West Virginia.

Name Spencer Don Identification Number _____ USES Number _____
    (Last Name) (1st Name) 2nd Name)

Address _____, Masontown State W.Va. County _____
    (Street and Number) (Village, City)

Date of Birth November 15 1914 Age last birthday 24 Yrs. Color: White x Negro ____ Other ____

Grade in school completed 1st, Yr. Hi School last attended Masontown High School.

WORK EXPERIENCE PRIOR TO CCC

Kind of Work Done	Time in Weeks	Employer's Name	Employer's Address	Employer's Business
Hauled Coal	12	Mr. Martin	Morgantown, W.Va.	Hauling Coal.
Laborer	24	RFC	Arthurdale, W.Va.	Labor
Clerk	20	A & P Tea Store	Masontown, W.Va.	Merchant
A&P Tea Store	20			

CAMP WORK EXPERIENCE

Title of Occupation (Specific Camp Job)	Occupational Code	Nature of Experience and Training (Just what the enrollee did in each occupation)	Time in Weeks
Road work.	8-0390	Pick and Shovel, (Unskilled labor).	32
Cabin Construction	7-0612	Use the Axe, Saw, and Hammer. (Rough Carpentry.)	28
Beautification Roadside	8-0390	Used Axe, Saw. (Unskilled Labor.)	32
Overhead	8-0390	General work in camp	4
S-75 Cabin Construction	7-0612	Used Axe, Saw, and Hammer.(Rough Carpentry)	48

COMMENT OF IMMEDIATE SUPERIOR ON QUALITY OF WORK

Occupation	REMARKS (Together with Name and Title of Foreman, Officer, etc.)
Carpentry	Pretty good Worker. Dependable. Quality of work is good. Does the Job right. Mr. Wiles.

General attitude toward work and the job: Interested in work, Does good work, and Dependable.

Signed: *John Wiles* Title: Junior Foreman

(OVER)

GENERAL INFORMATION

A. DISCHARGE INFORMATION

Kind of Discharge_____Honorable_____ Date__March 31_____1939___

Reasons for Discharge____Expiration of terms of Enrollment._____

Total Time Enrolled in this Company____12____Months, From__March 13_____1938____
to__March 31_____19 39___.

B. MISCELLANEOUS INFORMATION

Hobbies and Leisure-Time Interests:____Reading, and Swimming._____

TRAINING COURSES COMPLETED IN CAMP

TITLE OF COURSE	Hr./Week	No. Weeks	QUALITY OF WORK — REMARKS
History	1	48	Learned the history of the past, and present.
Elementary	1	48	Learned the XXX principals of mathematics.
English	1	48	Learned how to use the proper english.
Civics	1	48	Learned the Form of Gov't of the U.S.
Shorthand	1	48	Learned the principals of shorthand.
Log Cabin Construction	1	48	Lerned the constructions of log cabins.

Health Record:_____Good_____ Height__5__Ft.__2__in. Weight__135__Lbs.

Comments of Camp Educational Adviser: Interested in School work, and if given the opportunity
would like to go back to school. Dependabll.

Omar T. Goddin.

C. SUGGESTIONS FOR FUTURE COUNSELING, GUIDANCE AND PLACEMENT AND REASON FOR THESE SUGGESTIONS

Should be placed on some kind of a construction job as he is interested
in this kind of work and is capable of doing good work along this
kind of work.

_____
Project Superintendent

_____
Educational Adviser

_____
Company Commander

Life in the C.C.C.   By Marshall Davis   "Sunday Morning"   Life in the C.C.C.

Life in the C.C.C.   By Marshall Davis   "Sylvan Secret"   Life in the C.C.C   By Marsh

Life in the C.C.C.   By Marshall Davis   "Comin Round the Mountain"

Civilian Conservation Corps USA 20c
1933-1983

FIRST DAY OF ISSUE

LURAY, VA
APR
5
1983
22835

CIVILIAN CONSERVATION CORPS
1933 · 50TH ANNIVERSARY · 1983
1933 1942

NATIONAL ASSOCIATION OF CCC
DEDICATED TO THE PRESERVATION OF AMERICAN PRIDE · PRINCIPLE · PURPOSE · PROGRESS
U S
ALUMNI
EST 1977

Honoring
the CCC

Official First Day Cover

CIVILIAN CONSERVATION CORPS

50th Anniversary
of the Organization of
ROOSEVELT'S TREE ARMY
OFFICIAL FIRST DAY COVER

LURAY, VA
APR
5
1983
22835

Civilian Conservation Corps USA 20c
1933-1983

FIRST DAY OF ISSUE

Official
First Day
of Issue

LURAY, VA
APR
5
1983
22835

FIRST DAY OF ISSUE

Civilian Conservation Corps USA 20c
1933-1983

1882
1982
USA
20c
Franklin D. Roosevelt

50th Anniversary
Civilian Conservation Corps
1933-1983

ArtCraft

J. RIKER, USAF RET.
6072 Hudson Ave.
San Bernardino, CA 92404

CCC Artifacts

LARRY SYPOLT

-175-

 CCC TRIVIA

Well-known motion picture and television actor, Raymond Burr, was an enrollee at Camp Whitmore, California.

The Veterans Administration selected all war veteran enrollees.

If an enrollee was absent without leave more than eight days, he was given a dishonorable discharge.

Three days leave was granted in order for an enrollee to vote or register to vote in a primary or general election.

Camps were inspected periodically and rated. The best in a district was presented with a flag or banner.

If a junior enrollee got married while in the CCC, he could finish his enlistment but could not reenlist.

Hitchhiking or riding freight trains was prohibited.

It cost approximately $1,000 per enrollee per year in 1940 for food, clothing, overhead and allotments to dependents.

A typical enrollee was between 18 and 19 years old upon enlistment, had completed eight years of school, and had been without a job for seven months prior to entering the Corps. He weighed about 147 pounds, was 5'8¼" tall and served in the CCC from nine to 12 months.

The U.S. Department of Labor supervised the selection of enrollees but did not make the actual selection as it had no staff for it. The relief administration in each state made the actual selection. In 1939, the CCC administration took over direct selection of enrollees.

In 1933, almost three-quarters of the CCC camps were in national or state forests.

"We Can Take It" was the unofficial motto of the CCC used by enrollees through its nine-year history. Two camps at Broken Arrow and Keystone, Oklahoma were named Camp We Can Take It.

In March 1933, there were an estimated 13,600,000 people unemployed in the United States.

Before the CCC was established in 1933, many European countries such as Germany, Bulgaria, Switzerland, Austria, Poland, Czechoslovakia, the Netherlands, and Great Britain, as well as Canada and South Africa had established youth work camps.

The camp with the highest elevation was in Colorado at 9,200 feet above sea level while the lowest was in Death Valley, California, at 270 feet below sea level.

Twenty-five Federal government agencies participated in some capacity in the CCC.

⇑ EPILOGUE ⇑

This letter received from Rudy Polise, 1703 N. Fern-
wood Avenue, Pensacola, Florida, possibly sums up the
thoughts of the millions of men who served in the Corps.

I have always thought of the days I spent at High
Point (New Jersey, Company 1280, SP-8). Every time
I went north I swore that I would go back to see the
place where our camp was. Then something would
happen and I would have to put it aside till next time.
Well, last year (1979) I made up my mind that it was
Co. 1280 or bust Then after 40 years I was finally near-
ing High Point Park past Newton, then Franklin, then
I saw it in the distance. The High Point monument
standing 220 feet tall on the highest peak in New Jersey.
Then I got scared. I was afraid to go on, afraid of what
I would find or would not find. Perhaps after all these
years I traveled 1,400 miles chasing a dream. I started
to turn around and go back to Florida. But the group
I was with would not have any part of it. My wife said
that after hearing me talk about the CCC for 38 years
and getting so close there was no way for me to turn
back. Well, we turned at the stone house on the hill
and started down into the camp. The first thing I saw
was a toll booth in the middle of the road. It cost one
dollar to get in the state park. The bear cage was still
there. I guess the bear had to be a different one. Then
came Lake Marcia; the old ice storage house was gone.
Then the camp site came in view. The place had grown
up. There were picnic tables all over. All that was left
of the camp was some blocks that the barracks floor
sat on. We went to the monument. I rode over roads
that I helped build. We visited two artificial lakes that
the CCC boys built. The roads that looked so wide
while we were building them were now narrow but still
in good shape. The waterfalls or spillways we built by
hand out of large rock looked beautiful. Then as we
left, I felt sorry and glad at the same time. Sorry because
there was not one sign or anything telling tourists that
the roads they were riding on or the lakes they were
fishing in were built by a depression army. For this I
will always be sad. Then I felt glad and happy because
after all these years a part of me will always be at Co.
1280, SP-8, High Point Park, New Jersey. Then I had
no right to expect the camp and everything else to remain the same. Perhaps I went back there expecting
to find my youth again, or something to rekindle a fire
in a lamp that will for all outward purposes slowly dim,
then go out But until that light goes out, I will always
remember the time spent in the CCC.

BIBLIOGRAPHY

These are the more recent publications about the Civilian Conservation Corps.

1. Howell, Glenn, *CCC Boys Remember: A Pictorial History of the Civilian Conservation Corps*, Klocker Printery, Medford, Oregon, 1976.

2. Lacy, Leslie Alexander, *The Soil Soldiers, The Civilian Conservation Corps in the Great Depression*, Chilton Book Company, Radnor, Pennsylvania, 1976.

3. Lange, Howard L., *A Humanitarian Endeavor During the Great Depression*, Vantage Press, New York, 1984.

4. Merrill, Perry H., *Roosevelt's Forest Army, A History of the Civilian Conservation Corps*, Montpelier, Vermont, 1981.

5. Reynalds, Gerald. *The Woodpecker War*, Beck Printing, Clearwater, Florida, 1977.

6. Salmond, John A., *The Civilian Conservation Corps, 1933–1942, A New Deal Case Study*, Duke University Press, Durham, North Carolina, 1967.

7. Otis, Alison, William D. Honey, Thomas C. Hogg, Kimberly K. Lakin, *The Forest Service and Civilian Conservation Corps: 1933–42*, U.S. Department of Agriculture, Forest Service, 1986.

ABOUT THE AUTHOR

Since graduating from college in West Virginia in 1961 with a degree in geology, Stan Cohen has had many interests. In addition to being in the ski business as well as being both a director of a historical park in Montana and a consulting geologist. He now has his own publishing company in Missoula, Montana, where he lives with his wife, Anne. He has authored or co-authored 78 books since 1976 and published over 300.

THE CALIFORNIA CONSERVATION CORPS MUSEUM

Beautiful San Luis Obispo, on the central coast of California, is home to the Conservation Corps State Museum. Established Aug. 18, 1995, the museum is housed in four historic buildings that were part of Camp San Luis Obispo circa 1941. The museum honors the accomplishments of the young men and women who have served in conservation corps programs that have made a significant impact on California's natural resources and communities. The four buildings contain displays of artifacts and memorabilia related to the history and operations of all conservation corps programs that operated in California – past, present and into the future.

The Civilian Conservation Corps Building represents a typical CCC barracks building from the 1930s. It is complete with tools, uniforms and other artifacts.

The NACCCA Building houses a library and research center with over 100 binders containing photos and paper ephemera. It is open for public use.

The California Conservation Corps (CACC) Building is dedicated to documenting the achievements of the corps within California which was founded in 1976.

The Conservation Corps Institute (CCI) Building holds information concerning the youth corps movement of the 20th and 21st centuries.

The CCC Building of the Museum.

Interior scenes of the CCC Building.